THE BRAZILIAN KITCHEN

THE BRAZILIAN KITCHEN

100 CLASSIC AND CONTEMPORARY RECIPES FOR THE HOME COOK

Leticia Moreinos Schwartz

PHOTOGRAPHY BY BEN FINK

Published in 2010 by Kyle Books,
an imprint of Kyle Cathie Ltd.
www.kylebooks.com

Distributed by National Book Network
4501 Forbes Blvd., Suite 200
Lanham, MD 20706
Phone: (800) 462-6420 Fax: (301) 429-5746
custserv@nbnbooks.com

Text © 2010 Leticia Schwartz
Finished food photography © 2010 Ben Fink
Location photography on pages 1, 6, 7, 9, 10, 12-13, 44-45, 62-63,
114-115, 130-131, 145 © 2010 by Luciano Bogado
Location photography on pages 8, 24, 43, 53, 66, 71, 89, 96, 113, 152
© 2010 by Leticia Schwartz
Book design © 2010 Kyle Cathie Limited

Project editor Anja Schmidt
Designer Jee Chang, Black Paper Design
Food styling Susan Vajaranant
Prop styling Roy Finamore
Copyeditor Ann Cahn
Production Lisa Pinnell and Gemma Jordan

ISBN 978-1-906868-20-8

A cataloging-in-publication record for this title is available from
the Library of Congress

Color reproduction by Sang Choy
Printed and bound in Singapore by Tien Wah Press

CONTENTS

A MISSION OF JOY AND LOVE

Think of Brazil and you think of soccer, samba, bossa nova, beaches, and carnival. Brazilian food, however, is not yet as popular as our other assets. Many cookbooks group Brazil in the same pot as Latin American cuisine. But unlike the rest of South America, Brazil was colonized by Portugal, and our cuisine is represented by three different cultures: the Portuguese, the African, and the native Indian. The result is a delicious combination of exotic dishes prepared with techniques and ingredients from all three cultures meeting in the same pan. Brazilian cuisine is incredibly rich and deserves to shine on its own—that's what inspired me to write this book. This book is a celebration of my beloved Brazilian culture. Cooking the dishes I grew up on is the way I found to reconnect with my country after I left it, and my tribute to Brazil couldn't be contained to just the plates on my table.

The Brazilian Kitchen is based on a collection of classic Brazilian dishes with some inspirational recipes thrown in. My main goal with this book is to teach you something you don't know about Brazilian cuisine, and to inspire you to cook dishes you haven't considered trying before, evetunally incorporating this cuisine into your home kitchen just as you would with Italian, French, or Indian.

In addition to some of my favorites, I also tweaked some recipes to my taste. When I lived in Brazil, I loved many of these dishes the way they are traditionally made. But after 12 years of working as a chef in America, my palate has changed. Now I find the stews too heavy, the *petiscos* (bar foods) too big, and the sweets much too sweet.

There are a few demanding recipes, I'll confess, such as the Empadão de Frango on page 92, and to make it easier I like to prepare the dough and filling one day in advance and assemble them on the next day. But what strikes me about Brazilian cuisine is that there is always a casual feel and an elegant simplicity to our cooking that derives from our culture.

Growing Up in Brazil

I was born and raised in Ipanema, where life was good with the beach, cosmopolitan culture, parties, music, and lots of food. My upbringing in

Rio has always made me a proud *carioca* (a person born in Rio). My parents bought me my first recipe notebook when I was eight years old, and I still have it. I began writing in it with the first things I ever cooked—Pão de Queijo, fluffy little cheese breads (see page 16), and Brigadeiros, chocolate fudge balls (see page 132). At the age of fifteen, I started to think of the possibility of a career in the food business. I searched for cooking classes in Rio. There were not many, but I found Gracia Vienna, an Egyptian-born woman who had a passion for cooking and who was a great influence on my love of cooking.

In 1997, I moved to New York City to enroll at the French Culinary Institute. I loved the cu-

linary program so much that I stayed for the pastry program as well, taking night classes while interning at Le Cirque 2000. I staged under almost every station, but it was at the pastry station where all the buzz and glamour of cooking was happening, under master chef and chocolate king Jacques Torres.

Following graduation I continued my training at other French restaurants until marriage and kids brought on another move, this time to the suburbs of Connecticut, where I started my own cooking school and I continue to teach Brazilian classes all over the tristate area.

My husband, Dean, is American and so are my children, Thomas and Bianca. Dean always says that when you marry someone from another country, you marry the country. I couldn't agree more. In our house, we instill many Brazilian habits, and our kids are growing up on rice and beans, Pão de Queijo, yucca sticks, and brigadeiros. In my heart there are two countries now—America and Brazil. In addition to being a cookbook in itself, this book also represents the marriage of two cultures.

Brazil's food world today

The culture behind Brazilian gastronomy and food writing is very young. It's been only a decade or so since we started celebrating the chef as a profession in Brazil and cherishing our native ingredients. Until then, yucca, dendê oil, and so many other ingredients were seen as peasant food prepared by people who didn't rely on any written recipe. When asked to share these recipes the cooks would orally explain their guidelines, memories, and routines, and it was up to the listener to take notes.

Brazil has been adopted by many international chefs, who went to Brazil to work, fell in love with the country, and never left. One of the most esteemed chefs is Claude Troisgros, son of legendary chef Pierre Troisgros, owner of the restaurant Troisgros, in Roanne, France. After 27 years in Rio, Claude is now a *carioca* at heart, exploring exotic Brazilian ingredients combined with French techniques to create amazing dishes. In São Paulo culinary practi-tioners such as Emanuel Bassoleil and Laurant Sadeau are among others who have chosen Brazil as their new homes and realized what a huge resource it is with local ingredients.

For many years Rio de Janeiro and São Paulo were considered the two metropolitan areas that dominated tourism. This is no longer the case as other cities are becoming food destinations, such as Tiradentes in Minas Gerais, which now has a restaurant like Tulha Du Chef and gastronomic festivals. In Belém-do-Para, the capital of the state of Pará, chef Paulo Martins in his restaurant, Lá em Casa, is exploring the heart of the Amazon, using ingredients most of us have never even seen or heard of. In Bahia, the restaurant Tempero da Dada has attracted tourists from around the world.

It's so exciting to see the culinary landscape change. Brazilian-born chefs are now also working with Brazilian ingredients, such as Ludmilla Soeiro and Roberta Sudbrack in Rio, the above-mentioned Paulo Martins in Belem-do-Para, Carla Pernambuco, Ana Luiza Trajano, and Alex Atala in São Paulo, just to name a few. These chefs are creating amazing dishes such as Guava Paste Soufflé with Mascarpone Sauce (page 144), Yucca Sticks (page 34), and Baked Coconut (page 168). I am delighted to feature such contemporary recipes in this book. Now, when you think about Brazil, you won't just think of carnival and soccer. Trust me on this: You'll think food.

Bar Food
Petiscos

CAIPIRINHA

Refreshing, cool, sweet, and festive, *caipirinha* is Brazil. And if *caipirinha* is Brazil, then *cachaça* (see Glossary on page 170) is our national shrine. *Caipirinha* is a simple cocktail based on a mixture of mashed lime with sugar, ice, and *cachaça*. There are a few variables, however, that make all the difference. The lime should be cut into medium chunks, then mashed with sugar by a wooden muddler until the lime releases its oil. Transfer to a shaker, add some ice and *cachaça,* shake, and pour. Some recipes advise against mashing the lime too hard, as the oil can taste bitter. That's a very legitimate argument, but the sugar protects it and the more you release those oils, the better. Remember that *caipirinha* calls for lime and not lemon. Lemon skin is much thicker and carries a heavier white layer, giving a stronger bitter taste. I like my *caipirinha* on the lighter side, although it's very common to use a stronger dose than suggested here. *Caipirinha* is not the type of drink to serve out of a pitcher or prepare too far in advance. Each must be prepared individually, shaken individually, and immediately poured into a wide sturdy glass.

MAKES 1 CAIPIRINHA

2 limes
1 tablespoon sugar
2 to 3 tablespoons cachaça (adjust amount to taste)
Ice cubes

1   Trim the ends off the limes. Cut the limes into medium-size wedges.

2   Using a muddler, or the end of a wooden spoon, mash the limes with the sugar, making sure to squeeze all the juices from the lime and to dissolve the sugar in the juice.

3   Transfer the lime mixture to a shaker. Add the *cachaça* and ice cubes. Shake well (8 to 10 times) and pour into a large, but not tall, glass.

PLAYING WITH CACHAÇA

Use other citrus fruit to make *caipirinhas*, but keep in mind the white layer mentioned above; as long as you use a citrus with a thin skin—and that may vary from citrus to citrus—your *caipirinha* will taste great. Berries make a sweet and colorful drink as well. Strawberries? Call it Caipi-rubi. Vodka? Caipiroska. The ingredients below are also delicious.

Proceed with the caipirinha recipe at left, substituting the orange for the limes. Add the mint leaves to the shaker with the orange sugar mixture.

MAKES 1 CAIPIRINHA

1 orange
1 teaspoon sugar
2 tablespoons cachaça
4 to 5 mint leaves

CHEESE BREAD

Pão de Queijo

A soft chewy bread roll about the size of a golf ball infused with cheesy flavor, *pão de queijo* is Brazil's favorite savory snack and an excellent recipe to add to your repertoire. The manioc starch (see Glossary on page 170) is what gives the cheese bread an incredible gooey and chewy texture, so try your best to use both types of manioc starches. I always buy manioc starch in big quantities when I find it so whenever I decide to make *pão de queijo*, and that is quite often, I don't have to go hunting for it. A few online sources are www.ipanemagirl. net, www.amigofoods.com, www.sendexnet. com. The result is a softer batter and a slightly sweeter cheese bread that is still very delicious. You can prepare this recipe ahead of time and freeze the little rolls unbaked for up to 3 months. Just pop one in the oven directly from the freezer, and in 12 to 15 minutes you'll have deliciously cheesy treats!

2 cups finely grated fresh Parmesan
  (or Pecorino Romano)
2 large eggs
2 egg yolks
1¼ cup sour manioc starch (*povilho azedo*)
¾ cup manioc starch (*povilho doce*)
2 teaspoons kosher salt
½ cup whole milk
½ cup water
¼ cup plus 3 tablespoons extra virgin olive oil

1 Place the grated Parmesan in the bowl of a food processor. Add the eggs and yolks and blend until you have a smooth paste, about 1 minute. Set aside.

2 Place the two starches and salt in the bowl of an electric mixer fitted with the paddle attachment. Set aside.

3 Place the milk, water, and oil in a small saucepan, and bring to a boil. Immediately pour the milk mixture all at once into the starch mixture and turn the machine on at low speed. Mix until the dough is smooth and the starch is all incorporated, about 2 minutes.

4 Pause the machine and add the cheese and egg paste, scraping directly into the manioc starch mixture. Mix the dough at low speed until it turns a pale yellow, about 10 minutes. You are trying to develop the structure of the dough by kneading it slowly. The dough will feel a bit sticky.

5 Transfer the dough to a bowl, cover it with plastic wrap, and chill for at least 2 hours in the refrigerator.

6 Preheat the oven to 350°F. Line a baking sheet with parchment paper.

7 Wet your hands with olive oil (alternatively, you can flour your hands with manioc starch) and use an ice-cream scooper as portion control to make 1-inch balls, rolling them with your hands. Place them on the baking sheet, leaving about 1½ to 2 inches between each roll (or you can freeze them at this point by storing them in a zip-lock bag for up to 3 months).

8 Bake the cheese rolls in the oven until they puff up and look lightly golden brown, about 12 to 14 minutes. To ensure even baking, rotate the pan once during baking time.

9 Remove the baking sheet from the oven and place the rolls in a basket lined with a napkin. Serve immediately while they are still at their warmest and chewiest.

COD FRITTERS

Bolinho de Bacalhau

This is the granddaddy of bar foods served in *boutequins* all over Brazil. An exquisite deep-fried morsel that usually comes in a basket, cod fritters come in many variations. What makes this particular recipe so delicious and different are the egg whites mixed into the batter, which provide the fritters with a delicate, airy texture. When buying salt cod, try to find a piece that looks very meaty. Allow a bit of planning for this recipe since you need to soak the cod for at least 24 hours, preferably for 2 to 3 days. The cod is then gently poached in milk and cut into tender shreds before being mixed with the mashed potatoes. The result is a tender and fluffy cod-potato mixture surrounded by a golden crunchy crust. Once the fritters are done, they reheat quite nicely in the oven. I often serve this as hors d'oeuvres with tartar sauce, or as a main course with a green salad on the side.

1½ pounds salt cod (this will make 1½ cups
   of shredded cod)

3 cups milk

1 large Idaho potato

kosher salt and freshly ground black pepper

1 tablespoon finely chopped onion

2 cloves garlic, finely chopped

2 tablespoons fresh chopped parsley

4 large eggs, separated

1 tablespoon olive oil

½ teaspoon cayenne pepper

pinch of ground nutmeg

2 cups vegetable or canola oil, for deep-frying

1   Trim away all the dark parts around the belly and tail of the cod, then rinse it in cold water and place it in a large container. Fill it with about 2½ gallons cold water, and refrigerate for 2 to 3 days. Change the water at least 3 times per day, and each time you change the water, rinse the container as well.

2   Place the cod in a medium saucepan. Cover with the milk and gently bring it to a boil over medium heat. Reduce the heat to low and cook, uncovered, until it becomes opaque, 5 to 7 minutes.

3   Using a slotted spoon, remove the cod and break the meat with your hands into big chunks, then shred the meat by either chopping it with a chef's knife or pulsing it through a food processor. You should end up with about ½ pound (1½ cups) of shredded fish. Place the cod in an airtight plastic container and refrigerate until ready to use (the cooked cod will keep for up to 6 hours).

4   Peel the potato and cut it into chunks. Place the potato in a heavy-bottomed saucepan, cover with cold water, and add a pinch of salt. Cover the pan, bring the water to a boil, then reduce the heat to medium, and simmer until the potato is fork-tender, 8 to 10 minutes. Drain in a colander and, while still hot, pass the potato through a ricer or food mill.

5   In a large bowl, mix the shredded cod, mashed potato, onion, garlic, parsley, egg yolks, olive oil, and cayenne. Add the salt, pepper, and nutmeg to taste.

6   In a separate bowl, use an electric mixer fitted with the whisk attachment to beat the egg whites until they form soft peaks. Carefully fold the egg whites into the cod-potato mixture with a rubber spatula. You won't be able to shape the fritters with your hands since the dough is too light so you will need to spoon the batter directly into the hot oil.

7   Pour the vegetable oil into a heavy-bottomed pot and heat the oil to 350°F, as measured with a deep-fat thermometer. If you don't have a thermometer, drip a little batter into the oil—when you hear a sizzling sound and see the batter turning golden brown, the oil is ready. Drop a tablespoonful of batter into the oil and add only as many as will fit without touching. Turn occasionally with a long slotted spoon, making sure all sides are browned evenly, 2 to 3 minutes.

8   Remove each fritter from the oil and place it onto a baking sheet lined with a double layer of paper towels to absorb any extra oil. Continue working in batches until all the fritters are cooked—keep the finished batches in a warm oven until serving. Serve immediately. These can be reheated in a 300°F oven for 5 to 10 minutes.

QUAIL EGGS WITH KETCHUP SAUCE

Ovos de Codorna com Molho Rôse

It is very common in Brazilian restaurants to serve bread, butter, and other small accompaniments as soon as guests are seated at their table. One of my favorite foods of all the different types of accompaniments is quail eggs with red sauce. It's easy to make and very refreshing. The sauce can be prepared up to 3 days ahead of time.

MAKES 4 SERVINGS

1 box of 18 quail eggs

3 tablespoons mayonnaise

1 tablespoon, plus 1 teaspoon crème fraîche

2 tablespoons heavy cream

¼ teaspoon lime juice

1 teaspoon tomato paste

2 tablespoons, plus 1 teaspoon ketchup

salt and freshly ground black pepper

3 tablespoons fresh chopped chives, for garnish

KETCHUP VINAIGRETTE

While Molho Rosê is the perfect expression of tradition when eating quail eggs, you might consider trying this Vinaigrette as a lighter option. If you can't find maple vinegar, use apple cider or sherry vinegar instead.

2 tablespoons ketchup

⅛ cup maple vinegar

1 tablespoon minced shallot

⅓ cup extra virgin olive oil

1 In a bowl mix the ketchup, maple vinegar, and shallot.

2 Add the olive oil, slowly, in a steady stream while whisking all the time until it creates an emulsion.

3 This makes ½ cup.

1 Place the eggs in a medium saucepan and cover with cold water. Place over high heat and bring to a boil. Reduce the heat to low and simmer for 4½ to 5 minutes—you don't want to cook the yolks all the way through.

2 Using a slotted spoon, transfer the eggs to an ice bath. Let them chill until cool enough to touch, about 3 minutes. Peel each egg and place them in a bowl. Set aside.

3 Place the mayonnaise, crème fraîche, heavy cream, lime juice, tomato paste, and ketchup in a bowl, and whisk well until evenly blended. Season with salt and pepper.

4 Spoon some sauce on a plate and arrange the quail eggs on top. Sprinkle with the fresh chives.

RICE CROQUETTES WITH CAVIAR

Croquettes de Arroz com Caviar

While living in the United States, I heard about the rise of a chef named Alex Atala who is doing modern Brazilian cuisine at DOM, a restaurant located in São Paulo. I was not only happy to dine at DOM but proud to see a born and raised Brazilian chef praising our own ingredients with such towering ambition. The genius of his food is not its exotic flair but its clarity. One of Atala's simplest creations is the inspiration for this recipe. At DOM, it is topped with a small spoonful of caviar and I suggest you follow suit. But even plain, the croquettes are so good I am sure you'll munch on a few before the dollop of fish eggs.

MAKES 12 TO 15 CROQUETTES

1½ cups cooked white rice, cooled
½ cup freshly grated Parmesan
1 large egg
¼ cup whole milk
⅓ cup all-purpose flour
kosher salt and freshly ground black pepper
pinch of ground nutmeg
2 cups vegetable oil
1 to 2 ounces caviar

1   In a large bowl, mix together the rice, Parmesan, egg, milk, and flour. Season with the salt, pepper, and nutmeg. The batter should feel moist but firm. Using a tablespoon for portion control, form the batter into 12 to 15 croquette shapes.

2   Pour the vegetable oil into a heavy-bottomed pot and heat to 350°F, as measured with a deep-fat thermometer. If you don't have a thermometer, drip a bit of batter into the oil—when you hear a sizzling sound and see the batter turning golden brown, the oil is ready. Fry the croquettes in batches. Add as many as will fit without touching one another. Turn occasionally with a long slotted spoon, making sure the croquettes are browned evenly on all sides, 2 to 3 minutes.

3   Transfer to a baking sheet lined with a double thickness of paper towels to absorb any oil. Continue working in batches until all the croquettes are cooked. Keep the finished batches in a warm oven until serving.

4   Serve immediately with a dollop of cavier on each croquette. To reheat, place them in a 300°F oven for 3 to 5 minutes.

MEAT CROQUETTES

Croquettes de Carne

On our way to our country house in Teresópo-lis, a city one hour from Rio, my family used to stop on the highway at a roadside place called Casa Do Alemão. People line up to eat their famous croquettes, which I tried to replicate here. The recipe is quite simple and everything can be done ahead of time. You can make them small for hors d'oeuvres or a little bigger to be served as a main course with a green salad. The coating (flour, egg, and crumbs) provides texture and keeps the oil from pen-etrating the filling during frying. To achieve successful dredging, none of the items should be overcoated. I even use a dry pastry brush to dust them off, ensuring a very thin layer of flour. Once coated on all three items, fry the croquettes immediately so that the coating remains dry. Take the ground meat out of the refrigerator 20 to 30 minutes before using so it cooks more evenly and breaks into small bits of meat instead of big lumps.

1 cup veal stock

3 tablespoons unsalted butter

⅓ cup all-purpose flour

¾ cup diced onion

2 tablespoons olive oil

2 tablespoons minced garlic

1 pound ground beef

3 tablespoons tomato paste

1 teaspoon Worcestershire sauce

2 large egg yolks

kosher salt and freshly ground black pepper

1 teaspoon cayenne pepper

freshly ground nutmeg

1 cup flour

2 large eggs, lightly beaten

2 cups breadcrumbs

2 cups canola oil, for frying

1 Pour the veal stock into a medium saucepan and bring to a boil over medium heat.

2 Meanwhile, in a different saucepan, melt the butter over low heat.

3 Immediately add the flour to the butter and mix with a wooden spoon, cooking over low heat until the flour and butter become a roux, about 2 minutes. Add the veal stock all at once and cook over medium heat, whisking constantly until the milk thickens, about 3 minutes. Set aside.

4 In another saucepan, sauté the onion in the oil over medium heat, until soft and translucent, about 2 minutes. Add the garlic, and cook, while stirring, until it gets hot, about another minute. Add the ground beef and break it up with a wooden spoon into tiny bits until it is completely cooked, 3 to 5 minutes. Add the tomato paste and Worcestershire sauce and stir.

5 Pour in the reserved veal stock mixture and cook over medium heat, stirring constantly, for about 2 minutes. Season with salt, pepper, cayenne, and nutmeg, then add the egg yolks. Transfer to a flat tray and refrigerate for at least 2 hours, or overnight.

6 When the batter is completely cold, form it into croquette shapes. Place the croquettes in a single layer in an airtight container and refrigerate for 1 hour.

7 Prepare three different trays: one for the flour, one for the eggs, and one for the breadcrumbs. Pass each croquette through the flour, then the eggs, shaking the excess off each time. Coat it well with the breadcrumbs and shake off any excess.

8 Pour the canola oil into a heavy-bottomed pot and heat the oil to 350°F, as measured with a deep-fat thermometer. If you don't have a thermometer, drip a bit of batter into the oil—when you hear a sizzling sound and see the batter turning golden brown, the oil is ready. Fry the croquettes in batches, adding only as many as will fit without touching one another. Turn occasionally with a long slotted spoon, making sure they are browned evenly on all sides, 2 to 3 minutes.

9 Transfer onto a baking sheet lined with a double thickness of paper towels to absorb any extra oil, then keep warm. Serve immediately with Red Pepper and Brazil Nut Pesto (page 24). These can be reheated in a 300°F oven for 5 to 10 minutes.

RED PEPPER AND BRAZIL NUT PESTO

Pesto de Pimentão Vermelho e Castanha-do-Pará

MAKES 1½ CUPS

½ cup Brazil nuts

1½ cups red bell pepper, peeled, seeded,
and cut into chunks

1 red bird's eye chile (Pimenta Malagueta),
seeded and cut into chunks (optional)

1 clove garlic

¾ cup extra virgin olive oil

kosher salt and freshly ground black pepper

⅛ teaspoon paprika

⅛ teaspoon ground chipotle red pepper (optional)

1   Preheat the oven to 325°F.

2   Place the nuts on a baking sheet and roast them until they become fragrant, about 12 minutes. Remove from the oven and let them cool completely at room temperature before using.

3   Place the nuts, red pepper, chile, if using, garlic, and 1 tablespoon of the olive oil in a food processor and process until finely ground.

4   With the processor running, pour the remaining olive oil in a thin steady stream to create an emulsion. Season with the salt and pepper, paprika, and chipotle, if using.

5   To serve, transfer the pesto to a bowl. Pesto will keep in an airtight container in the refrigerator for up to 3 days.

BAKED CHEESE CRACKERS

Sequilhos de Queijo

I learned this recipe when I was 15 years old from Gracia Vienna, a cooking teacher from whom I took my first official cooking course in Rio. This recipe has remained a snacking mainstay for me ever since. I still love the taste of the beautiful golden cheese crust, the buttery flavor, and the crumbles around the edges. I like to serve it in soups and salads or simply with a good glass of wine. Best of all, you can put the dough together in less than 5 minutes.

MAKES ABOUT 45 CRACKERS

1¼ cups, plus 1 tablespoon all-purpose flour, sifted
1 stick, plus 6 tablespoons unsalted butter, cut into cubes, lightly chilled
½ teaspoon salt
1½ cups finely grated Parmesan
1½ cups finely grated Gruyère

1   Preheat the oven to 350°F. Line a baking sheet with parchment paper.

2   In a food processor, process the flour and butter until the dough begins to come together. Add the salt and two cheeses and process until it is just blended, about 1 minute. Be wary of overworking the flour or incorporating air into the dough.

3   Transfer the mixture to a lightly floured surface and form it into a ball. Wrap it in plastic wrap and refrigerate for at least 1 hour (or up to 3 days; you can also freeze the dough for up to 2 months).

4   Remove the dough from the refrigerator and using a small ice-cream scoop or a melon baller, make 1-inch balls. Press each gently between the palms of your hands to flatten it just a little, as you would with a cookie.

5   Arrange the crackers on the prepared baking sheet, leaving a 1-inch space between them. Bake until the crackers are lightly golden brown, 13 to 15 minutes, rotating once.

6   Remove the baking sheet from the oven and transfer the crackers to a wire rack to cool. Eat them slightly warm or at room temperature. Store the crackers in an airtight plastic container in the refrigerator for up to 5 days. To reheat them, place a batch on a baking sheet in a 350°F oven for 3 to 4 minutes.

PUMPKIN FLAN WITH JERK MEAT SALAD

Flan de Abóbora com Salada de Carne Seca

Anyone who's ever eaten in a *botequim* has surely tasted *Purê de Abóbora com Carne Seca*—mashed pumpkin purée with jerk meat. Seeking to lighten the dish and add a flash of luxe, I turned the recipe into a pumpkin flan topped with a warm *carne seca* salad and dressed with a pumpkin-seed vinaigrette.

This is quite easy to make and can be prepared ahead of time. In the United States, there are a cornucopia of alternatives to pumpkin: Butternut squash and acorn squash are the most familiar. Just be sure you use a hard squash for this recipe.

MAKES 6 TO 8 SERVINGS

FOR THE FLAN

2 tablespoons canola oil

3 tablespoons unsalted butter

1 pumpkin (weighing about 3 pounds), peeled, seeded, and cut into 1-inch cubes (about 6 cups)

¼ teaspoon freshly grated nutmeg

⅛ teaspoon ground cinnamon

kosher salt and freshly ground black pepper

5 cloves garlic, roughly chopped

4 large eggs

2 cups heavy cream

FOR THE MEAT

½ pound jerk meat

1 small onion, peeled and halved

1 small carrot, peeled

1 stalk celery

1½ cups veal stock

1 plum tomato, peeled, seeded, and diced

1 cup frisée lettuce

2 tablespoons mayonnaise

2 tablespoons fresh chopped chives

FOR THE VINAIGRETTE

¼ cup extra virgin olive oil

5 cloves garlic, finely minced

¼ cup shelled pumpkin seeds, unsalted

2 tablespoons sherry wine vinegar

pumpkin-seed oil to garnish

6 to 8 four-ounce ramekins or a metal muffin pan

1 Preheat the oven to 300°F. Grease the ramekins lightly with canola oil.

2 Melt the butter in a large skillet over medium heat. Add the pumpkin and stir until all the pieces are hot and coated in butter. Add the nutmeg and cinnamon. Season lightly with salt and pepper. Cover the pan and reduce the heat to low. Cook, stirring occasionally. When the pumpkin is fairly soft, 5 to 7 minutes, add the garlic and stir. Cover and cook until soft and tender, 15 to 20 minutes. Close to the final minutes of cooking, uncover the pan to allow the excess moisture in the pumpkin to evaporate.

3 Transfer the pumpkin and garlic to a food processor fitted with the steel blade and process until smooth, about 1 minute. Add the eggs and heavy cream. Season with salt and pepper, pulsing to combine the spices.

4 Ladle the custard into the ramekins. Set the ramekins in a shallow roasting pan in the oven. Pour warm water into the pan until the sides of the ramekins are covered halfway, 4 to 6 cups of water. Bake until the custard is set, 35 to 40 minutes.

5 Remove the roasting pan from the oven. Place the ramekins on a rack to cool to room temperature. Chill in the refrigerator for another 3 hours before unmolding. You can prepare this up to 3 days ahead and store in the refrigerator, covered with plastic wrap.

6 Meanwhile, prepare the jerk meat. Trim any extra fat from the meat and soak it in cold water in the refrigerator for 24 hours, changing the water 3 times at regular intervals.

7 Place the meat in a medium saucepan and pour in enough fresh cold water to cover the meat by at least 2 inches. Bring the water to a boil, then replace the water with fresh cold water again. Repeat this process 3 times.

8 Transfer the meat to another pan with the onion, carrot, and celery. Cover with the veal stock. Simmer at low heat, covered, until very tender, about 2 hours.

9 Remove the meat from the liquid and let it cool to room temperature. This can be done up to 2 days ahead; just leave the meat in the liquid inside an airtight plastic container.

10 Using your hands, pull the meat into thin shreds and place it in a bowl. Discard any fat. Add the tomato, frisée lettuce, mayonnaise, and chives and toss lightly.

11 To make the vinaigrette, place the oil in a small heavy skillet, and cook the garlic and pumpkin seeds over low heat, until the garlic starts to turn golden, about 2 minutes. Stir in the vinegar. Season with salt and pepper.

12 To serve, reheat the pumpkin flans in a 225°F oven for 12 to 15 minutes. Unmold the flans by inverting each ramekin in the center of a plate, arranging the meat salad on top of the flan, and dividing the vinaigrette sauce among the plates. Drizzle some pumpkin-seed oil around each flan and serve warm.

CARNE SECA

As Brazilians like to use a pressure cooker for everything, we often use one for *carne seca*, to make it soft and tender. Braising is a perfect alternative, and can be done up to two days ahead of time, but keep the meat in the braising liquid. If you cannot find *carne seca*, substitute any strong flavored smoked meat or even a country ham, as long as the pulled meat is full of flavor.

FLATBREAD TOPPED WITH VATAPÁ

In this recipe, the traditional Brazilian fish pureé *vatapá* finds a new role: sauce for a pizza. It can be spread just like tomato sauce on top of a flatbread, which is then topped with shrimp, dendê oil, hearts of palm, and tomato. This pizza-style preparation is a fun dish that is easy to prepare, great for entertaining, and surprisingly light. Making the flatbread is quite easy and it can be prepared ahead of time, but you can substitute ready-bought pizza dough. Just be sure to roll it very thin, otherwise the dish will become a bit too heavy.

FOR THE DOUGH

1¾ cups all-purpose flour, sifted, plus extra
  for dusting

¼ teaspoon baking soda

½ teaspoon kosher salt

4 tablespoons unsalted butter, cut into pieces

⅓ cup cold water (a little more or a little less
  depending on humidity)

2 tablespoons olive oil

2 cups chilled Vatapá (page 78)

1 vine tomato, thinly sliced

¼ cup thinly sliced hearts of palm

6 medium shrimp, peeled and deveined

kosher salt and freshly ground black pepper

3 tablespoons dendê oil

2 tablespoons fresh chopped cilantro

1   In the bowl of a food processor, combine the flour, baking soda, and salt. Add the pieces of butter and pulse until the mixture becomes a coarse meal.

2   With the machine running, add the water in a steady, thin stream. The dough will start to shape into a ball. Before it actually holds its shape, turn the dough onto a lightly floured surface. Using your hands, gather the dough into a ball. If necessary, add a little more flour. Knead the dough by hand, or in a mixer fitted with the hook attachment, until the dough looks smooth, about 5 minutes.

3   Cut the dough in half and wrap each piece separately with plastic wrap. Chill for at least 30 minutes in the refrigerator.

4   Preheat a grill or place a grill pan over medium-high heat.

5   On a lightly floured surface and using a rolling pin, roll one piece of dough into an 8-inch circle, between ¹⁄₁₆ and ⅛ inch thick, lifting the dough often and making sure the work surface and the dough are amply floured at all times. Wipe off any excess flour on top of the dough and brush the olive oil over the top side.

6   Carefully lift the dough, being sure to keep it in one piece, and place it with the olive oil side down on the grill or grill pan. Using a pair of tongs, lift the dough to check for grill marks and that the dough is completely cooked on the bottom, about 2 minutes. Slide the dough onto a wire rack with the uncooked side up. Cool for 5 to 10 minutes.

7   Preheat the oven to 350°F.

8   Spread the Vatapá on top of the uncooked side, leaving an edge of ½ inch (as you would with a pizza). Arrange some tomato slices, hearts of palm, and shrimp on top. Season the entire surface with salt and pepper, then drizzle some dendê oil over it.

9   Bake the flatbread in the oven until the shrimp is cooked and the flatbread is nice and crunchy, 5 to 7 minutes.

10 Remove it from the oven and garnish with the cilantro. Slice into 6 pieces and serve immediately.

BEAN FRITTERS

Acarajé

This fritter is probably the biggest symbol of African culture in Brazil. For over two centuries fritters have been sold in the streets of Bahia, a large state on Brazil's eastern coast, as a snack. *Acarajés* look like big oval meatballs with a reddish brown crust and a grainy soft bean purée on the inside, and one really is a meal in itself. I wanted to prepare this famous fritter in a smaller version while still keeping its authenticity. Dendê oil (see Glossary on page 170) can be rather expensive in the States so I use half dendê and half canola oil. (If you use only canola oil, the fritters won't reach their beautiful reddish color.) The batter is prepared with uncooked beans as they will cook when they are fried. If you use cooked or canned beans, the batter will simply melt away in the oil. These *acarajés* can stand up to lots of hot seasoning.

1 cup black-eyed beans
½ cup diced onion
kosher salt and freshly ground black pepper
pinch of cayenne pepper
pinch of Spanish paprika
2 cups canola oil
2 cups dendê oil

1 Place the beans in a bowl and cover them with tap water.

2 Leave the beans to soak at room temperature uncovered, for at least 12 hours, preferably 24 hours, changing the water at least once (or anytime you see that the water has turned brown). Discard any floating shells.

3 Drain the beans and spread onto a baking sheet lined with paper towels so that they air dry completely, about 5 minutes. Place the beans in a food processor with the onion. With the machine running, add some salt and pepper, cayenne, and paprika and process until finely ground.

4 Pour the canola and dendê oils into a large heavy-bottomed pot or casserole and heat the oil to 350°F, as measured with a deep-fat thermometer. If you don't have a thermometer, drip a bit of batter into the oil—when you hear a sizzling sound and see the batter turning golden brown, the oil is ready. Using two oval-shaped teaspoons, make little quenelles by scooping a bit of batter and transferring it from one spoon to another, putting some pressure against the spoons as you create the shape of a quenelle. Drop the quenelles directly into the hot oil. Add only as many as will fit in the oil without touching one another. Turn occasionally with a long slotted spoon, making sure all the sides are browned evenly, about 3 minutes.

5 Transfer the fritters onto a baking sheet lined with a double thickness of paper towels to absorb any extra oil. Continue working in batches until all the fritters are cooked. Keep the finished batches in a warm oven, until serving. Serve immediately with a side of *vatapá* (page 78). These can be reheated in a 300°F oven for 5 to 10 minutes.

BEAN FILLINGS

Black-eyed beans or black-eyed peas are the original bean used in this recipe, but you can also use navy beans. In Bahia, acarajés are served with other fillings such as caruru (made with okra, dried shrimps, coconut, cashews and peanuts), or a simple salad of red onions, tomatoes, cucumbers and bell peppers. Feel free to play with other fillings as well.

YUCCA CROQUETTES

Croquettes de Aipim

Yucca is one of the most important vegetables in Brazil from a historical, cultural, economic, and nutritional perspective. In this recipe, yucca is used as Mother Nature intended, raw and naked, and transformed into a crispy finger food—another *botequim* classic. The crunchy outside provides a nice contrast to the smoothness of the mashed yucca. The center, filled with a small piece of blue cheese, pairs beautifully with the flavor of yucca. If you are not a fan of blue cheese, use another kind of cheese, such as Minas, goat cheese, mozzarella, Parmesan, Manchego, or provolone. Mashing yucca takes a bit more elbow work than mashing potatoes.

MAKES ABOUT 20 CROQUETTES

2 pounds yucca

3 tablespoons unsalted butter, softened

1 large egg yolk

kosher salt and freshly ground black pepper

pinch of ground nutmeg

5 ounces Gorgonzola, coarsely crumbled

FOR THE COATING

1 cup flour

1 large egg, lightly beaten

2 cups panko breadcrumbs

2 cups canola oil, for frying

1. Cut off the ends of the yucca and make 3 to 4 vertical cuts from top to bottom with a paring knife. Peel the two layers of the vegetable: the brown skin and the inner white layer. Cut the yucca in half lengthwise and remove the center woody fiber with a paring knife. Cut the white flesh into 1-inch chunks.

2. Transfer the yucca to a medium saucepan, cover with fresh cold water by at least an inch, and add a good pinch of salt. Cover and bring to a boil. Reduce the heat to medium and cook until tender, 15 to 20 minutes.

3. Drain the yucca and, while still hot, pass through a food mill or ricer. Immediately add the butter and egg yolk, mixing vigorously until well blended. Season with the salt and pepper and nutmeg.

4. Flour your hands. Form tablespoon-size balls. Gently press a dent into each ball and insert a small piece of cheese in the very center of each croquette. Bring the dough up and around the cheese as you close and seal the edges. Shape the balls into croquettes.

5. Prepare three trays for the flour, egg, and panko breadcrumbs. Pass the croquettes through each and shake off any excess.

6. Follow the deep-frying instructions (steps 8 and 9) as for the Meat Croquettes on page 23.

FRIED EMPANADAS

Pastel de Carne Seca com Catupiry

MAKES ABOUT 20 EMPANADAS

FOR THE JERK MEAT

½ pound jerk meat

1 small onion, peeled and halved

1 small carrot, peeled

1 stalk celery

1½ cups veal stock

¾ cup catupiry cheese

4 cups vegetable oil, for frying

FOR THE DOUGH

1¼ cups all-purpose flour

1 teaspoon salt

¼ teaspoon baking powder

2 tablespoons extra virgin olive oil

¼ cup, plus 3 tablespoons sparkling water

1 tablespoon vodka

From fillings of meat to cheese, seafood to poultry, the *pastel*, or empanada in English, is a treasured *botequim* food. In this recipe I use a very Brazilian filling of jerk meat and *catupiry* (see Glossary on page 170). In Brazil, there are several brands of ready-made dough available, and you can certainly find them in the United States. Any other braised meat can replace the jerk. If you cannot find *catupiry,* substitute cream cheese or a triple creamy cheese such as Sainte-André, Brie, or Explorateur.

1 Prepare the jerk meat as instructed in steps 6–10 (until mixing with tomato, etc.) on page 27, then mix it with the catupiry cheese in a bowl and set aside, or store in the refrigerator in an airtight container for up to 2 days.

2 To prepare the dough, sift together the flour, salt, and baking powder and place in the bowl of an electric mixer fitted with the paddle attachment.

3 Mix the olive oil, sparkling water, and vodka in a separate bowl. Turn the machine on at low speed and pour the liquid over the dry ingredients in a steady stream, until the dough gathers into a ball and the sides of the bowl are completely clean, about 1 minute.

4 Turn the machine off, change the attachment from a paddle to a hook, and knead the dough until it's very smooth and elastic, about 10 minutes. Depending on the humidity, you might need to add more flour. Flour your hands and form the dough into a ball. Wrap it in plastic wrap and chill for at least 30 minutes or up to 2 days. Bring back to room temperature before proceeding.

5 Cut the dough in half and keep the piece you are not using wrapped in plastic to prevent it from drying out. On a lightly floured surface, roll the dough as thin as possible. With a 3-inch round cookie cutter, stamp out as many circles as possible, 6 to 8. Reroll the scraps and stamp out more.

6 Working with one round at a time, fill each circle with 2 teaspoons of stuffing. Lightly brush the edges with water and fold the dough over into a half-moon shape. Crimp the edges with a fork to seal. Cover the assembled ones with plastic wrap while you work on the other half of the dough.

7 Deep fry as per steps 8 and 9 on page 23.

YUCCA STICKS

Biscoito Palito de Povilho

I grew up with an addiction to beach snacks. Among my favorites was *biscoito globo*, a round yucca cracker about the size and shape of a bagel. The flavor is quite mild, but it's the light crunchiness that draws munchers. These are sold in supermarkets in Brazil with lots of variety in shape but little in flavor. Recently however, during one of my trips to Rio, I went to Claude Troisgros's restaurant Olympe. He serves a fun and creative version of the cracker with a light touch of curry that is absolutely addictive. My experimentation with this recipe at home went through a few structural transformations, and finally my cracker became a stick. You can serve these as a snack or a light appetizer. Pair them with Red Pepper and Brazil Nut Pesto (page 24) or another dip and serve with a Caipirinha (page 14). You can also substitute lemon zest for orange zest and thyme for rosemary. Although I use kosher salt inside the batter, feel free to use another kind of salt for sprinkling, such as sea salt or pretzel salt. This recipe only works with the true Brazilian ingredient, sour manioc starch (*povilho azedo*).

1½ cups sour manioc starch (*povilho azedo*)

1 cup water

1 tablespoon whole milk

1 teaspoon kosher salt, plus more for sprinkling

8 tablespoons (1 stick) unsalted butter, softened, at room temperature

1 large egg

1 tablespoon, plus 1 teaspoon fresh chopped rosemary

zest of 1 orange

freshly ground black pepper

¼ cup extra virgin olive oil

¼ teaspoon ground chipotle pepper, plus more for sprinkling

1 Preheat the oven to 350°F. Line two baking sheets with parchment paper.

2 Place the manioc starch in the bowl of an electric mixer fitted with the paddle attachment.

3 Bring the water, milk, and salt to a boil in a small saucepan. Immediately pour the hot liquid over the manioc starch and beat at a low speed, until the mixture looks like a coarse meal, about 1 minute. Add the butter and beat until the dough is smooth and the sides of the bowl are clean. Add the egg, 1 tablespoon of the rosemary, orange zest, and two to three twists of freshly ground black pepper. Beat the mixture until the dough turns pale and creamy, 3 to 4 minutes.

4 Stop the machine and scrape the dough into a resistant pastry bag fitted with a plain round tip, size number 3. Pipe the yucca sticks into 6-inch lengths onto the baking sheet, leaving about ½ inch between each stick. It is important to pipe the sticks quite thin as they expand during baking time. (Alternatively, you can roll them by hand, on a surface lightly floured with manioc starch. Roll one piece at a time into a 6-inch long stick, then transfer them to the baking sheet.) Lightly brush the sticks with olive oil and sprinkle some salt, rosemary, and a dust of chipotle pepper over each.

5 Bake in the oven until they rise and turn slightly golden, 25 to 35 minutes. Turn the oven off, open the door all the way, and leave inside for another 30 minutes.

6 Remove the baking sheets from the oven and let cool for 10 minutes. Place the sticks in a tall glass and serve.

COOKING TIPS

A few little tricks you should follow to achieve success with this recipe: Bake the sticks immediately after the dough is prepared, or the dough will dry out before baking and crack in the oven. Once they are baked and puffed, leave them inside the oven with the oven off and the door all the way open for at least 30 minutes. Otherwise, they will be hard like toffee. The more ventilation they receive, the crunchier they become, so if you have a convection mode in your oven, be sure to use it. Although these can be stored in a plastic container for 3 to 4 weeks, they tend to lose crunchiness with humidity and time, so before serving, reheat them in a 225°F oven for 20 to 25 minutes.

STUFFED CRAB SHELLS
Casquinha de Siri

In Brazil we have a different species of crab, but I think the American variety, especially the Maryland blue, is one of the best in the world—meatier and sweeter—and because of this I like to make this recipe more often in the United States than in Brazil. I love to serve this dish in a seashell. Most of the time, I use scallop shells instead of the original crab shells, but if you don't have a sea creature shell available, just use a porcelain ramekin. This is a fantastic recipe for entertaining because it can be completely assembled ahead of time.

1   Place the bread in a bowl, pour the coconut milk over, and let soak for 10 to 20 minutes while you prepare the other ingredients.

2   Pick over the crabmeat to remove any excess shell and set aside.

3   In a medium saucepan, warm the olive oil over low heat. Add the onion and the yellow and green peppers and cook, stirring occasionally, until they are soft and tender. Add the garlic and cook for another minute, until it is tender. Add the tomatoes and cook for another minute, until they get hot. Add the wine and reduce it by half, 1 to 2 minutes. Add the bread and coconut milk and the grated coconut. Cook, stirring, until everything starts blending together, about 3 minutes.

MAKES 6 TO 8 STUFFED SHELLS

1 cup diced white bread, crusts removed
1 cup coconut milk
1 pound jumbo lump crabmeat
2 tablespoons extra virgin olive oil
⅓ cup chopped onion
½ cup diced yellow pepper
½ cup diced green pepper
3 cloves garlic, minced
½ cup diced tomatoes
¼ cup dry white wine
¼ cup unsweetened grated coconut
1 teaspoon mustard
1 teaspoon fresh lemon juice
2 tablespoons unsalted butter
2 tablespoons fresh chopped cilantro
kosher salt and freshly ground black pepper
¼ teaspoon Old Bay seasoning

FOR THE CRUST
2 tablespoons unsalted butter
½ cup manioc flour (*farinha de mandioca*)
kosher salt and freshly ground black pepper
¼ cup grated Parmesan
Maldon Sea Salt or kosher salt, for garnish

4   Turn off the heat and add the crab, mustard, and lemon juice. Fold everything together. Some pieces of crab will naturally shred, but try to keep some big lumps. Add the butter and cilantro. Season with salt and pepper and Old Bay. If your mixture looks dry, add 1 or 2 tablespoons of coconut milk or wine. Transfer to a bowl and let cool completely. This can be done up to two days ahead and kept in an airtight container in the refrigerator.

5   Meanwhile, prepare the crust. Preheat the oven to 350°F.

6   In a medium saucepan, melt the butter over medium-low heat. Add the manioc flour and stir constantly, toasting the flour until it reaches a light golden color. Watch carefully so that the flour does not burn. Transfer to a bowl and season with salt and pepper. Let cool for 5 minutes, then add the Parmesan and mix it in evenly.

7   Divide the crab mixture into the scallop shells. Spread a thin coat of crust on top. Place the stuffed shells onto a baking sheet and bake in the oven until the filling is hot and the crust is a light golden brown, 12 to 14 minutes.

8   To serve, place a small pile of Maldon Sea Salt on the bottom of a soup plate and place a shell on top.

PINEAPPLE MANCHEGO
SKEWERS

Abacaxi Picante com Manchego no Palito

This is a very simple appetizer with an undeniable elegance, perfect for a last-minute get-together. It's refreshing and perfectly balances the soft, sweet pineapple and the firm, nutty, salty Manchego—Spain's most famous sheep's milk cheese. In Brazil, I made this dish with Gouda, but once I tried it with Manchego, I never looked back. Look for an aged cheese, which will have a deep, buttery feel. To make a nice presentation, cut the fruit and the cheese into perfect squares of the same size. Save the trimmings for another recipe, or just snack on them like I do. Try to find some nice-looking skewers because this presentation relies on the sum of its very few parts. I like the bamboo ones sold in Asian specialty stores.

=== **MAKES ABOUT 20 SKEWERS** ===

½ pound fresh pineapple, peeled
6 ounces Manchego, at room temperature
2 tablespoons sugar
1 tablespoon water
2 tablespoons salted butter
⅛ teaspoon ground cinnamon
⅛ teaspoon ground chipotle
kosher salt and freshly ground black pepper
20 small bamboo skewers

CHOOSING CHEESE

This appetizer lends itself to many different types of cheeses and is a great way to try something new since you don't need to buy a lot. Cheeses that can be used instead of Manchego are Roncal or Queso Zamorano from Spain, or Terrincho Velho from Portugal.

1 Cut the pineapple into ½-inch cubes using a serrated knife. Cut the Manchego into cubes about the same size. You should have about 20 pineapple cubes and 20 Manchego cubes.

2 Place the sugar in a small skillet and add the water. Cook over high heat until it turns into a light amber color, 2 to 3 minutes. (Since this a very small quantity it can be easily overcooked, so watch carefully.)

3 Add the butter and swirl the pan around. Everything will splash and bubble, so be careful. When the butter is well blended with the caramelized sugar, turn the heat to low and add the cinnamon and chipotle. Cook the caramel, whisking constantly, until it gets a little thicker, about 2 minutes.

4 Add the pineapple squares and swirl the pan around, allowing the pineapple to caramelize in the sauce and become lightly golden brown, but don't let it get too mushy, 3 to 4 minutes. Season with salt and pepper.

5 Pour the pineapple and sauce onto a flat plate. While the fruit is still hot, place a piece of pineapple on the skewer, then a piece of Manchego. Place the skewers on a serving plate and serve immediately, while the pineapple is still warm.

CHICKEN FRITTERS

Coxinha de Galinha

Coxinha, "little drumstick" in Portuguese, is a typical street food—the dough is stuffed with shredded chicken and catupiry cheese, then deep-fried. The "little" label is inaccurate in my opinion. The old kitchens of Brazil make this delicious fritter too doughy and too big. One of my best friends and mentors, Patty Pulliam, shares my sentiments. A true connoisseur of Brazilian cuisine, she recently developed this ingenious recipe. It has all the grace of a *coxinha* and the finesse of a small appetizer: a crunchy and thin crust, a moist chicken filling, and an elegant sauce. Patty suggests thigh meat for this recipe, it being the most succulent part of the chicken, but really you can use any leftover chicken. Traditionally, a pinch of turmeric is added to the dough.

MAKES 8 TO 10 FRITTERS

FOR THE FILLING
1 tablespoon extra virgin olive oil
¼ cup finely minced shallot
2 cloves garlic, finely minced
1 pickled sweet red pepper, drained
    and finely chopped
kosher salt and freshly
    ground black pepper
1 cup shredded cooked chicken,
    packed tight
1 tablespoon mayonnaise
3 tablespoons fresh chopped
    chives

FOR THE DOUGH
1 cup, plus 2 tablespoons chicken
    stock
½ teaspoon extra virgin olive oil
1 teaspoon kosher salt
⅛ teaspoon turmeric (optional)
1 cup all-purpose flour, sifted,
    plus extra to knead

FOR DREDGING
1 cup flour
2 large egg whites, lightly beaten
1 cup breadcrumbs
2 cups canola oil, for frying

FOR THE CHEESE SAUCE
1½ cups chicken stock
1½ cups catupiry cheese *
kosher salt and freshly ground black
    pepper
2 tablespoons fresh chopped chives
extra virgin olive oil to drizzle

* Catupiry cheese can be found in Brazilian grocery stores or visit www.chefleticia.com for shopping sources.

1 Prepare the filling. Warm the olive oil in a medium skillet over low heat. Add the shallot and cook, stirring, until soft and translucent, 1 to 2 minutes. Add the garlic and cook until it is hot, about 1 minute. Add the red pepper and season with salt and pepper. Transfer to a plate and let cool for about 10 minutes.

2 In a large bowl, place the shredded chicken and mix in the cooled shallot mixture, the mayonnaise, and chives. Season with salt and pepper. Let cool. (The filling can be prepared up to 1 day ahead and stored in an airtight plastic container in the refrigerator.)

3 Meanwhile, prepare the dough. In a medium saucepan, place the chicken stock, olive oil, salt, and turmeric, if desired, and bring to a simmer over low heat. When the stock is hot, add the flour all at once while stirring. A light crust will form on the bottom of the pan. Keep stirring—with vigor—for another minute to dry the dough.

4 Transfer the dough to an electric mixer fitted with the hook attachment and knead until it becomes soft and smooth, about 5 minutes. Scrape onto a floured surface and finish kneading the dough by hand, making sure your hands and the work surface are well floured. Form the dough into a flat disk and let rest at room temperature for 5 to 10 minutes before you start assembling the fritters.

5 Using a rolling pin, roll out the dough until it's about ⅛ inch thick. Using a 3½-inch cookie cutter, cut disks of dough and place them on a baking sheet lined with parchment paper. You will have some scraps that you can gather and reroll. You should be able to make 8 to 10 of the 3½-inch disks.

6 Using a tablespoon, scoop some filling in the center of each disk. To make the classic drumstick shape, use two lightly oiled hands, fold the dough up and around the filling into a beggar's purse, and gently press the filling down into the center as you close, pinching and sealing the edges. Pull the dough at the top out slightly so that it resembles a drumstick or an elongated chocolate kiss. Keep a moist towel close at hand to clean your fingers each time they touch the filling. Make sure the dough is not cracked; if it does crack, wet your fingers in water and pinch the dough together.

7 Prepare three different trays for the flour, egg whites, and breadcrumbs. Pass the fritters through each, shaking off any excess.

8 Pour the canola oil into a heavy-bottomed pot and heat to 350°F, as measured with a deep-fat thermometer. If you don't have a thermometer, dip a corner of a fritter into the oil—when you hear a sizzling sound, the oil is ready. Fry the fritters in batches. Turn occasionally, making sure all sides are browned evenly, 3 to 4 minutes.

9 Transfer to a baking sheet lined with a double thickness of paper towels to absorb any excess oil. Keep the finished batches in a warm oven until serving.

10 Prepare the cheese sauce. In a medium saucepan, bring the stock to a simmer over low heat. Add the cheese and whisk it slowly and constantly until it melts completely. Season with salt and pepper.

11 Pour the sauce in a bowl and garnish with the chives and a drizzle of olive oil. Serve the fritters alongside.

KIBBE

Kibbe de Carne

Brazil is a melting pot that received an influx of immigrants in the mid-1900s, including Lebanese, who brought along all sorts of wonderful foods. Kibbe has certainly worked its way into our culinary vernacular over the years, and it is a favorite of mine. For this recipe, make sure to buy very lean ground meat. If the meat is marbled with fat, the kibbe might not hold its shape when frying. Take the ground meat out of the refrigerator 20 to 30 minutes before using, so that it blends more evenly with the bulghur. Bulghur is a very nutritious grain and easy to work with. It has to soak in hot water before it is used. If the bulghur has too much liquid after soaking, make sure to drain it and dry it, or the kibbe will be mushy. I like to shape these about 3 inches long, but if you want to serve them as a main course, shape them a little larger. I love the accompanying Yogurt Mint Sauce, but feel free to serve kibbe with other sauces, such as mustard sauce or chimichurri.

MAKES 45 TO 50 KIBBE

1 cup finely ground bulghur
1 pound lean ground beef
½ cup finely chopped onion
¼ cup finely chopped scallion (white and green parts)
2 cloves garlic, finely minced
1 teaspoon dried oregano
¼ cup fresh chopped mint leaves
4 tablespoons extra virgin olive oil
2 teaspoons kosher salt
freshly ground black pepper
pinch of cayenne
a few drops of Tabasco Pepper Sauce
2 cups canola oil

1 Rinse the bulghur with warm water to remove any dirt and excess starch. Drain it in a colander and place it in a bowl.

2 Meanwhile, bring 4 cups of water to a boil and pour it over the bulghur. Cover the bowl with a tight lid or aluminum foil and soak the bulghur until it has expanded and tripled in size, 45 minutes to an hour.

3 Place the ground beef in a large bowl. Add the soaked bulghur, then stir in the onion, scallion, garlic, oregano, mint, and olive oil. Mix well with your hands until well blended. Season with the salt, pepper, cayenne, and Tabasco Pepper Sauce and mix again.

4 Start forming oval shapes by first rolling a tablespoon of mixture in a circular motion between the palms of your hands, then forming two pointed ends. (You can store the kibbe in an airtight container in the refrigerator for 1 day. Make sure to bring to room temperature at least 30 minutes before frying.)

5 Pour the canola oil into a heavy-bottomed pot or casserole and heat the oil to 350°F, as measured with a deep-fat thermometer. If you don't have a thermometer, dip one kibbe into the oil—when you hear a sizzling sound, the oil is ready. Fry the kibbe in batches. Add only as many as will fit without touching one another. Turn occasionally with a long slotted spoon, making sure they are browned evenly on all sides, 3 to 5 minutes.

6 Transfer onto a baking sheet that's been lined with a double thickness of paper towels to absorb any excess oil. Continue working in batches until all the kibbe are fried. Keep the finished batches in a warm oven until serving. Serve immediately. These can be reheated in a 300°F oven for 5 to 10 minutes.

YOGURT MINT SAUCE

MAKES 1 CUP

½ cup plain low-fat Greek yogurt
½ cup sour cream
1 tablespoon Dijon mustard
1 tablespoon finely chopped red onion
a few drops of fresh lemon juice
a few drops of Tabasco Pepper Sauce
kosher salt and freshly ground black pepper
2 tablespoons fresh chopped mint

1 In a medium bowl, whisk together the yogurt, sour cream, and mustard.

2 Stir in the red onion, lemon juice, and Tabasco Pepper Sauce.

3 Season with salt and pepper.

4 Add the mint and fold it in with a spatula. This sauce can be prepared up to 3 days in advance.

Salads and Soups
Saladas e Sopas

CRUNCHY MINAS CHEESE WITH TOMATO AND PESTO

Salada de Minas Crocante com Tomate e Pesto Brasileiro

Minas cheese is the muse cheese of Brazil. Originally from the state of Minas Gerais, hence the name, this pure white colored cheese has an incredible farm freshness, and a very humble pedigree, considering its popularity. The taste is a cross between feta, ricotta, and mozzarella. Like other fresh white cheeses, Minas has a way of complementing other flavors without masking them. See the Glossary on page 170 for more on Minas cheese. For this recipe, Minas cheese is covered in a panko crust, cooked in olive oil until it becomes lightly golden brown, and paired with tomato bruschetta and Brazilian pesto. If you can't find Minas cheese, you can use another white cheese, such as ricotta salata, queso blanco, or even goat cheese. The tomatoes can be prepared a few hours ahead, but the cheese should not be coated and cooked until just before serving. During the summer months, serve this with gorgeous heirloom tomatoes or with just a fresh green salad and a good vinaigrette.

MAKES 6 TO 8 SERVINGS

⅓ cup Brazil nuts
1 clove garlic, plus 2 cloves, minced
1 cup fresh parsley, preferably flat-leaf Italian
1 cup fresh cilantro
¾ cup extra virgin olive oil, plus 1 tablespoon
kosher salt and freshly ground black pepper
pinch of cayenne pepper
6 plum tomatoes, peeled and seeded
1 large shallot, finely chopped

½ cup flour
1 large egg, lightly beaten
1 cup panko breadcrumbs
1 pound Minas cheese
1 cup olive oil

8 to 10 ounces arugula, for garnish

1 Preheat the oven to 325°F.

2 Roast the nuts on a baking sheet until they just start to develop an aroma, about 12 minutes. Remove from the oven, transfer to a plate, and cool completely. Rub the nuts between your hands or use a cloth to peel away the thin brown skin. It should come off quite easily.

3 Place the nuts, garlic clove, herbs, and ¼ cup of the olive oil in a food processor. Pulse until blended. With the machine running, add the remaining olive oil (save 1 tablespoon)

in a steady stream. Season with the salt and pepper and cayenne. Store in an airtight container in the refrigerator for up to 3 days.

4   Chop the tomatoes and place them in a bowl. Mix in the shallot and minced garlic. Season well with salt and pepper. Drain out the tomato juices. Transfer the tomatoes to a bowl, add the 1 tablespoon of olive oil, and mix with a rubber spatula.

5   Prepare three different trays for the flour, egg, and panko breadcrumbs.

6   Cut the Minas cheese into ½-inch slices, then, using a 2-inch cookie cutter, cut circles out of the cheese. Pat the cheese dry with a paper towel. Pass each piece of cheese

through the flour, egg, and breadcrumbs, shaking off the excess in between.

7   Heat the olive oil in a large sauté pan on medium heat. Carefully add the cheese circles and cook on each side until lightly golden brown, about 2 minutes per side. Using a perforated spatula, remove the cheese rounds from the pan and transfer them to a plate or a baking sheet lined with a double sheet of paper towels.

8   To serve, place a mound of tomatoes on a plate, drizzle the pesto sauce around it, and top with a warm Minas cheese. Garnish with a few leaves of arugula.

GRILLED MINAS CHEESE WITH A BRAZILIAN PESTO SAUCE

Minas Grelhado com Pesto Brasileiro

This glorious appetizer requires very little work. The cheese is warm from the grill, but its firm texture keeps it from melting completely. Make sure you buy the whitest and freshest Minas cheese so that the grill marks appear, and try to use a grill or pan with a small grill elevation to prevent the cheese from sticking to the surface. Cutting the cheese into triangle shapes gives this dish a fancier look, but if you don't want to spare any cheese, leave it in the original round shape and enjoy those extra few nibbles. A combination of Brazil nuts with parsley and cilantro give this pesto a Brazilian wallop that is charming but not overwhelming.

MAKES 4 TO 6 SERVINGS

⅓ cup Brazil nuts
1 clove garlic
1 cup parsley leaves
1 cup cilantro leaves
¾ cup extra virgin olive oil
pinch of cayenne pepper
kosher salt and freshly ground black pepper

14 ounces firm Minas cheese
2 tablespoons extra virgin olive oil

1 Preheat the oven to 325°F.

2 Prepare the pesto as per steps 2 and 3 on page 47.

3 Place a grill pan over high heat on the stove, or preheat a gas grill.

4 Trim the round Minas cheese into a square. Cut the cheese in half diagonally to make 2 large triangles. Cut each large triangle in sections to make 4 to 5 thinner triangles, about ½ inch thick. Brush each triangle slice with olive oil and season with just a tiny pinch of salt (not too much since Minas cheese is already salted) and pepper.

5 Grill the cheese until you see medium-browned grill marks on both sides, being careful not to let the cheese melt, about 2 minutes on each side. Carefully transfer each triangle to a serving platter.

6 Spoon the pesto (which should be slightly cold or at room temperature) over the cheese and serve.

CHICKEN SALAD WITH STRING POTATOES

Salpicão de Frango

The best part of this salad is that it's an extraordinary dish from very ordinary kitchen ingredients: chicken, carrots, onions, potatoes, tomato sauce, and raisins. With the right treatment to each one of them, they become a chicken salad like you've never had before. You'll need a whole chicken for this recipe, but you can also adapt the recipe if you have leftover chicken. Try to resist cutting the chicken with a knife when you pull it. It's the textural juxtaposition of the hand-pulled chicken mixed with the carrots and crunchy potatoes that takes this dish to the next level. The thinner you pull the chicken, the better it will taste. Did I mention that you can make everything ahead of time? And the variations are endless—after Thanksgiving, try making it with turkey and cranberry.

MAKES 6 TO 8 SERVINGS

2 Idaho potatoes
1 quart vegetable or canola oil, for frying
salt
1 (3 to 4 pound) roasted chicken
2 tablespoons olive oil
2 cups thinly sliced onion
¾ cup dark raisins
2 tablespoons white wine
½ cup mayonnaise
3 tablespoons tomato sauce, preferably marinara
kosher salt and freshly ground black pepper
⅛ teaspoon cayenne
⅛ teaspoon paprika
2 cups coarsely grated carrots
2 tablespoons fresh chopped parsley

---

1. Cut the potatoes into a julienne cut, using a mandoline, or do it by hand. Place the potatoes in a bowl of cold water as you cut them, but change the water at least once, washing away any starch. Spread the potatoes onto a baking sheet lined with paper towels, and let them air-dry for 5 minutes.

2. Pour the oil into a large heavy-bottomed pot and heat to 350°F, as measured on a deep-fat thermometer. If you don't have a thermometer, dip one potato into the oil—when you hear a sizzling sound, the oil is ready. Fry the potatoes in batches until they are lightly golden brown. Transfer onto a plate lined with a double thickness of paper towels and immediately season with regular (not kosher) salt. Set aside. You can prepare the potatoes up to a day ahead; just be sure to keep them in an airtight plastic container at a dry room temperature.

3. To prepare the salad, pull the meat off all parts of the chicken by hand. (Discard the bones or use them for a chicken stock.) The thinner the meat, the better. You should have about 4 cups of pulled chicken. Set aside.

4. Place the olive oil in a large skillet and cook the onion over low heat, stirring occasionally, until they are soft and translucent, 10 to 15 minutes. (Resist the temptation to turn the heat to high, otherwise the onion will brown.) Transfer to a bowl and set aside.

5. In a small saucepan, over low heat, cook the raisins in the wine, just until soft, 3 to 5 minutes. Transfer the raisins with any remaining wine to a plate to cool and set aside.

6. In a medium bowl, mix together the mayonnaise and tomato sauce. Season with the salt and pepper, cayenne, and paprika.

7. In a big bowl, mix together the pulled chicken, onion, raisins, carrots, mayonnaise sauce, tomato, and parsley. Taste to adjust the seasoning. You can store the salad in an airtight plastic container in the refrigerator for up to 2 days, but bring it to room temperature 20 to 30 minutes before serving.

8. Place the salad on a large platter and arrange the string potatoes on top. For a fancier presentation, use individual ring molds, and press the salad inside. Remove the ring and garnish with potatoes on top.

ROASTING A CHICKEN

To roast your own chicken, preheat the oven to 400°F. To truss a chicken, cut a 3-foot piece of twine. Position the chicken breast side up with the neck toward you. Center the twine underneath the tail and loop it around the tips of the drumsticks. Cross the ends of the twine above the chicken, pulling it tight to close the cavity. Pull the twine down so it embraces the breasts and wraps down around the wings. Pull it tight again and knot the twine. Season the chicken with salt and pepper and place it in a roasting pan. Roast in the oven until it's done (the breast should be cooked to about 155°F and the legs to about 165°F, both as measured by a meat thermometer, 40 to 45 minutes. Remove the chicken from the oven, cut the twine off, and wait until the chicken cools to room temperature before pulling the meat.

SALTED AND PEPPERED MELON

Melão com Sal e Pimenta, Molho de Manga e Pimentão Amarelo

A perfect piece of melon that I enjoyed on a hot day in Rio is the inspiration for this recipe. Sweet and juicy melon marries quite well with savory foods and it takes the pepper and fleur de sel right in. The mango and yellow pepper sauce is a perfect complement to the lushness of the melon. In the United States, the orangy-pink flesh of the cantaloupe and its firm creamy texture makes it the perfect melon to receive a quick sear in the skillet. However, the abundance of melons available today are too varied to lock you into only one kind, so feel free to use other types of melons. But be careful when choosing melons, especially when they have been shipped over a long distance. I've been quite disappointed at times with rock hard melons that are practically tasteless. So be sure to make this recipe when good melons are in season during the summer.

MAKES 4 TO 6 SERVINGS

4 tablespoons extra virgin olive oil, more for drizzle
1 small shallot, chopped
1 yellow bell pepper, chopped
1½ cups chicken stock
1 ripe mango, cut into small chunks
kosher salt and freshly ground black pepper
1 ripe small melon (2 to 2½ pounds)
fleur de sel
1½ ounces mâche, trimmed, washed, and dried

1 Heat 2 tablespoons of the olive oil in a medium saucepan over medium heat. Add the shallot and yellow bell pepper and cook, stirring occasionally, until they are soft and translucent, about 3 minutes. Add the chicken stock and bring to a simmer. Cook until reduced by half, 5 to 6 minutes. Add the mango chunks and cook until they get hot and mushy, about 2 minutes. Season lightly with salt and pepper.

2 Transfer to a blender and blend until smooth. Strain the sauce through a fine sieve and directly into a bowl. Set aside. The sauce can be done up to 3 days ahead of time and stored in an airtight plastic container in the refrigerator.

3   Using a sharp knife, trim the peel from the melon. Cut it in half lengthwise and scoop out the seeds. Slice each half lengthwise into 4 to 5 spears, for a total of 8 to 10 spears, depending on the size of the fruit. Each spear should be 1 to 1½ inches thick. Season one side only with pepper.

4   In a large skillet, heat the remaining 2 tablespoons of olive oil over high heat. Add a few spears of melon, and cook on the peppered side only, until a nice caramelized crust develops. Don't crowd the pan. If neces-sary, do it in batches. Using tongs, carefully transfer the spears to a platter. Sprinkle a few crystals of fleur de sel onto each spear on the seared side of the melon.

5   Place 2 spears of melon on each plate with the seared side up, and carefully drizzle the mango sauce, which should be served at room temperature or slightly chilled, around the spears. Arrange a mound of mâche leaves on the plate and lightly drizzle them with olive oil and season with salt.

MANGO, SMOKED SALMON, AND ARUGULA SALAD

Salada de Manga e Salmao Defumado com Rucula

This recipe is inspired by a dish I used to make when I worked at La Caravelle, one of New York City's greatest temples of French haute cuisine. At that time, the young and talented chef Cyril Renaud prepared a smoked salmon and mango napoleon layered with crème fraîche that was so naturally sweet and refreshing that it always made me think of Brazil. Here, I use the same key ingredients in a salad. The buttery slices of sweet mango are inserted between salty smoked salmon and arranged over a bed of peppery arugula, then topped with a simple and tangy vinaigrette sauce. In each bite you can taste the contrast of sweet, salty, and peppery, making this salad intensely flavored and quite elegant.

2 tablespoons fresh lemon juice

1 teaspoon Dijon mustard

1 tablespoon crème fraîche

⅓ cup extra virgin olive oil

1 tablespoon canola oil

kosher salt and freshly ground black pepper

5 ounces baby arugula

1 medium ripe mango, peeled, pitted, and cut into
thin strips

5 ounces thinly sliced smoked salmon, cut into
strips, preferably fresh

1   Place the lemon juice, mustard, and crème fraîche in a food processor or blender. Pulse until well blended.

2   In a measuring cup with a spout, mix the two oils, then with the processor running, pour in a steady stream into the crème fraiche. Season with salt and pepper. This vinaigrette can be prepared up to 3 days ahead of time and stored in an airtight plastic container in the refrigerator.

3   Just before serving, place the arugula in a large bowl and pour just enough dressing over the leaves to coat and toss. Be careful not to overdress the leaves or they will turn mushy quite fast.

4   Place the arugula leaves on individual serving dishes and arrange the slices of mango and salmon on top. Lightly drizzle more vinaigrette on top and serve immediately. Store any extra vinaigrette in an airtight plastic container in the refrigerator for up to 1 week.

SHOPPING FOR MANGO

The mango is an exceptional fruit, full of pulp, flavor, aroma, texture, juice, and sweetness. It is the second most consumed tropical fruit, after the banana. The mango tree originated in India and was first brought to Europe, Africa, and the Americas by Portuguese explorers in the 18th century. The tree adapted particularly well to the climate of Brazil. Today, mangos are available year-round in most supermarkets. There are over 500 varieties, but the most popular ones are Golden Globe, Keitt, Tommy Aitkins, and Champagne Mango (in Portuguese known as Manga Carlota). Feel free to use any kind of mango for this salad, as long as the fruit is perfectly ripe (always press the fruit with your thumb; it should feel slightly soft). It pairs splendidly with the smoked salmon and arugula.

CURRIED CHICKEN SALAD

Salada de Galinha ao Curry com Amendoas e Passas

Chicken salad is an American staple and a Brazilian one, too. This salad is among the most flavorful approaches to the classic that you'll find, whether you use leftover chicken or with meat cooked just for this purpose. This salad is among the most flavorful approaches to the classic that you'll find. The presence of almonds, raisins, and cooked onion with curry and turmeric adds both crunchy and sweet elements to the chicken salad. It makes a great buffet dish or a small lunch served with a green salad on the side, and it's quite easy to prepare. Although you can make this recipe in just half an hour, it tastes even better the next day. I have been making this dish for about 15 years and I still get asked for the recipe every time I make it.

MAKES 2 TO 4 SERVINGS

⅓ cup golden raisins
2 tablespoons white wine
1 tablespoon olive oil
½ small onion, finely diced
2 cloves garlic, minced
1 teaspoon curry
1 teaspoon turmeric
1 cup chicken stock
⅓ cup almonds, lightly toasted and roughly chopped
2 cups cubed cooked chicken (light and dark meat)
3 tablespoons mayonnaise
2 tablespoons fresh chopped parsley
1 tablespoon store-bought balsamic vinaigrette
kosher salt and freshly ground black pepper

1 Cook the raisins in the wine in a small saucepan over low heat, just until they are soft, 3 to 5 minutes. Transfer the raisins and any remaining wine to a bowl, let cool, then set aside.

2 In another small sauté pan over low heat, cook the olive oil and onion, stirring occasionally, until soft and translucent, 2 to 3 minutes. Add the garlic, curry, and turmeric and continue stirring and cooking until they are hot, about 1 minute. Add the chicken stock and cook at a low simmer, letting it reduce by 80 percent, about 5 minutes. Be sure not to let the onion dry out.

While still wet, transfer the curried onion to a plate and let cool to room temperature.

3 In a big bowl, mix the raisins, curried onion, almonds, chicken, mayonnaise, parsley, and balsamic vinaigrette. Mix everything well until the salad is well blended.

4 Season with salt and pepper. At this point you can either serve this immediately or store in an airtight plastic container in the refrigerator for up to 3 days.

BRAZILIAN CHICKEN SOUP

Canja de Galinha

Some dishes are universal, with a slight regional variation. Matzo ball soup, chicken noodle soup, wonton soup—whether it's Jewish, American, or Chinese, all of these dishes are comforting. Here is the Brazilian version. This soup is so simple that it inspired a slang word in Portuguese: When something is "Canja," it means it is easy. The basic ingredients are chicken, rice, and *mirepoix* (onion, celery, and carrots). I like to add some asparagus in Spring. Cook the chicken gently without letting it come to a boil to create a meat that is succulent and tender. I love how the rice infuses the soup with starch and the chicken skin infuses the liquid with natural fat. I love to eat this soup with the Baked Cheese Crackers on page 25.

with the Baked Cheese Crackers on page 25.

MAKES 6 TO 8 SERVINGS

1 whole chicken (about 3½ pounds)
kosher salt and freshly ground black pepper
3 cups chicken stock
3 carrots, peeled and cut small on a bias
3 stalks celery, peeled and cut small on a bias
1 onion, thinly sliced
1 cup white rice
8 asparagus, peeled and cut small on a bias

1   Wash the chicken well with cold water, making sure to clear the inside cavity, removing any liquid and organs from the chicken. Season with salt and pepper and place in a large soup casserole. Cover with chicken stock, add 3 to 4 cups of water, and cover. Bring to a boil over medium to high heat and skim any foam that may form. Reduce the heat to low and gently simmer, covered, until the chicken is cooked through, 25 to 35 minutes (remember, don't let it boil at any point).

2   Using a pair of tongs, remove the chicken from the water, shaking any liquid from the chicken into the pan, and transfer to a plate. Cool to room temperature.

3   Add the carrots, celery, onion, and rice to the liquid. Lightly season with salt and pepper and simmer at low heat until the vegetables are tender and the rice is cooked through, 15 to 20 minutes.

4   Meanwhile, pull the chicken meat into thin threads and add them back to the soup. Discard the bones (or save them for stock) and skin.

5   A few minutes before serving, add the asparagus to the soup and simmer until just cooked, 3 to 4 minutes. Taste the soup, season again if necessary with salt and pepper, and serve hot.

PORTUGUESE SOUP
Caldo Verde

This classic soup is a full meal in itself, satisfying in every season. In Portugal they like to use a very green cabbage called Couve Gallego, but in Brazil this soup became a classic using couve mineira, otherwise known as collard greens. You can also use kale. Some recipes call for starchy potatoes, like the Idaho variety, which are then puréed with the chicken stock. I think a young potato adds a more delicate flavor and I prefer to smash just a tiny portion of potatoes. It will all depend on the quality of chicken stock you are using. If your stock is very watery, thickening the soup by smashing some of the potatoes will work well. If your chicken stock is nice and thick, that won't be necessary. In either case, this soup is easy to prepare and quite nourishing.

4 tablespoons olive oil

1 large onion, diced

3 cloves garlic, minced

1¼ pounds small yellow potatoes, peeled and cut into ½-inch chunks

1½ quarts Chicken Stock (page 112)

¾ pound pork sausage (Linguiça or Chorizo, see Glossary on page 170)

½ pound collard greens (or kale)

kosher salt and freshly ground black pepper

pinch of cayenne pepper

1 Place 3 tablespoons of the olive oil and onion in a large soup pot, over low heat, and cook until soft, stirring occasionally, 5 to 7 minutes. Add the garlic and cook until hot, about 1 minute. Add the potatoes and cook, stirring occasionally, until they get hot, about 4 minutes. Add the chicken stock. Cover the pot and bring the soup to a boil, then lower the heat and simmer gently until the potatoes are just cooked and fork-tender, about 15 minutes.

2 In the meantime, in a medium sauté pan over medium heat, add 1 tablespoon of olive oil and sauté the sausage, turning frequently, until nicely browned on all sides, about 5 minutes. Transfer to a flat plate lined with paper towels.

3 Scoop out 2 tablespoons of the potatoes, place them on a plate, and mash them completely with a fork. Return the mashed potatoes to the soup. Remember, the amount of potatoes you mash and add will affect how thick the soup will be.

4 When the sausage is cool enough to handle, cut into slices a little thinner than ½ inch. Add to the soup, cover, and cook at a gentle simmer for 5 minutes.

5 In the meantime, trim the thick stems from each leaf of the collard greens (or kale) and cut the leaves into a fine chiffonade. Add the greens and cook at a gentle simmer for another 5 minutes. If you want to prepare the soup ahead of time, hold the collard greens and add them 5 minutes before serving, as they are what will establish the bright green color that gives Caldo Verde its name.

6 Season the soup with salt, pepper, and cayenne. Serve in deep soup bowls.

CHICKEN STOCK

Making chicken stock can be quite impractical. However, stock can be part of your cooking on a semi-regular basis by simply using the leftover trimmings of a chicken. I never toss carcasses from roasted chickens because they make an excellent stock and they freeze very well. Some specialty stores sell fresh stock—that should be your second best option. If canned or boxed chicken stock is your only option, no problem, the soup is well worth making. Just be careful when seasoning, as canned stock tends to be saltier than fresh stock. See page 112 for a stock recipe.

YUCCA AND COCONUT SOUP WITH BAY SCALLOPS

Sopa de Aipim e Coco com Vieiras

One of the most rewarding aspects of cooking is creating new recipes by taking flavors that work well in a classic dish and cooking them with another technique. With this soup I rethought the flavor combination of yucca and coconut. This combination could not be more classically Brazilian, but it is rarely served as a soup. The yucca really strikes an earth tone in a way that no other root vegetable can achieve. The coconut milk adds a creamy texture that comes without any cream at all. The delicacy of bay scallops must, of course, not be overcooked. And, finally, it is so easy to prepare.

MAKES 4 SERVINGS

2 tablespoons dendê oil

1 medium onion, diced

3 cloves garlic, coarsely chopped

½ ounce fresh ginger, peeled and coarsely chopped

1 yucca (see page 32 for preparation)

3 plum tomatoes, quartered

¼ cup dry white wine

3⅓ cups chicken stock

1 cup coconut milk

1 tablespoon tomato paste

kosher salt and freshly ground black pepper

½ pound bay scallops

2 tablespoons extra virgin olive oil

2 tablespoons fresh finely chopped chives

1　In a medium saucepan, heat the dendê oil over low heat and add the onion. Cook, stirring occasionally, until it becomes soft and translucent, 3 to 5 minutes. Add the garlic and ginger and stir. Add the yucca, stirring until it gets hot, about 2 minutes. Add the tomatoes and stir well. Add the wine and reduce almost completely.

2　Add the chicken stock, coconut milk, and tomato paste and stir well. Season with salt and pepper and bring to a simmer, uncovered, over medium to high heat. Reduce the heat to low, cover, and simmer gently until the yucca is completely cooked, 15 to 20 minutes.

3　Working in batches, purée the soup in a blender. As each batch of soup is puréed, pour directly into a strainer set over another saucepan. Discard the solids. Season the soup with salt and pepper.

4　Pat the scallops dry and season with salt and pepper. Cook them in the olive oil in a medium sauté pan over medium heat, until they just start to turn opaque, about 2 minutes.

5　Reheat the soup if necessary and ladle it into warm bowls. Divide the scallops among each and garnish with the fresh chopped chives.

PUMPKIN AND COCONUT SOUP

Sopa de Abóbora com Côco

2 tablespoons extra virgin olive oil

1 3-pound pumpkin, peeled, seeded, and cut into
   1-inch cubes

3 small carrots, coarsely chopped

kosher salt and freshly ground black pepper

2 onions, coarsely chopped

4 cloves garlic, coarsely chopped

¾ cup white wine

3 to 4 cups chicken stock

2 cups coconut milk

2 tablespoons butter

2 tablespoons fresh chopped chives, for garnish

Like peas and carrots, pumpkins and coconuts are great pals. This very Brazilian partnership is traditionally seen in sweets and pastries, especially in jams sold in glass jars. I use it as another source of inspiration for a simple and casual soup. In terms of technique, it is similar to the classic American pumpkin soup, but the coconut milk adds a creamy and tropical flavor that elevates the pumpkin. If you'd like to add some texture, feel free to garnish the soup with lightly toasted pumpkin seeds or lightly toasted coconut or both.

1 In a medium saucepan, heat the olive oil over medium heat and add the pumpkin and carrots. Season very lightly with salt and pepper and cook, stirring occasionally, until they start to soften, about 5 minutes. Be careful they don't turn brown.

2 Add the onions and continue to cook, stirring occasionally until they start to soften, about 3 minutes. Add the garlic and let it get hot, about 1 minute. Add the white wine and let it reduce almost completely, about 3 minutes.

3 Add the chicken stock and bring to a boil. Add the coconut milk and bring to a boil again. Season lightly with salt and pepper and reduce the heat to low. Cover the pan and gently simmer the soup until the pumpkin and carrots are completely cooked, 15 to 20 minutes.

4 Remove the pan from the heat. Working in batches, purée the soup in a blender. As each batch of soup is puréed, pour it directly into a strainer set over another saucepan. Discard the solids. Add the butter and whisk well. Taste the soup and adjust the seasoning with salt and pepper.

5 Garnish with the chives and serve with the Baked Cheese Crackers on page 25.

Main Courses
Pratos Principais

BRAZILIAN FISH STEW

Moqueca de Peixe

This fish stew couldn't be more Brazilian, but with the presence of wine and fish stock, it has an international appeal that is hard to resist. *Moqueca* is originally from the state of Bahia, and there are many versions: fish, shrimp, or crab are the most popular. Use this recipe as a guideline and experiment with different types of fish, such as wild striped bass, halibut, and tilapia. (Be sure to buy Chilean sea bass from a sustainable fishery as the species recently had a close brush with extinction.) *Moqueca* is often served with *farofa* (see page 128), but feel free to use white rice as a side dish as well. With just a little bit of coconut milk, this colorful fish stew is rich only in looks and spirit—one spoonful will reveal how unbelievably light it is.

1 scallion (white and green parts), chopped

1 small onion, chopped

1 small piece fresh ginger, peeled and finely chopped

4 large cloves garlic, minced

5 tablespoons dendê oil

2 tablespoons extra virgin olive oil

4 tablespoons freshly chopped cilantro

1¼ pound sea bass, cut into 2-inch chunks

½ cup freshly chopped green pepper

⅓ cup freshly chopped yellow pepper

1½ cups fish stock

1 cup coconut milk

2 tablespoons tomato paste

1 tablespoon lemon juice

kosher salt and freshly ground black pepper

⅓ cup canned or jarred hearts of palm,
 drained and diced

2 plum tomatoes, peeled, seeded, and diced

1 Prepare the marinade for the fish: In a bowl, mix together half of the scallion, half of the onion, half of the ginger, and half of the garlic. Add 2 tablespoons of the dendê oil, all of the olive oil, and half of the cilantro. Place the fish chunks in a ziplock bag and add the marinade. Rub it around the fish so it is well distributed. Remove all the air from the plastic bag and seal it well. Place the fish in the refrigerator, making sure it is covered by the marinade, and let it rest for at least 3 hours.

2 Take the fish out of the refrigerator 30 minutes before using. Preheat the oven to 350°F.

3 Place 3 tablespoons of dendê oil in a large sauté pan over medium heat. Add the remaining scallion, onion, and the green and yellow peppers, and cook until they are soft, about 3 minutes.

4 Add the remaining ginger and garlic and mix well. Cook for another minute or until it's hot. Add the fish stock and let it come to a full boil. Add the coconut milk and tomato paste and let it come to a full boil, then lower the heat to simmer the sauce nice and gently.

5 In the meantime, spread the fish and marinade in a gratin dish. Pour the lemon juice on top and season lightly with salt and pepper. Bake in the oven until almost done, 10 to 12 minutes.

6 Carefully transfer each chunk of fish into the pan with the sauce. Pour in any remaining juices from the fish and marinade. Braise the fish in the sauce over low heat with the pan covered, until the fish is soft and tender, 5 to 8 minutes.

7 Uncover the pan, add the hearts of palm and tomatoes, and let them get hot.

8 Taste the sauce, then season it with salt and pepper and sprinkle with the remaining fresh cilantro. Serve over rice or farofa.

HEARTS OF PALM

Hearts of palm, or palmito in Portuguese, are harvested from the inner core of certain palm trees such as juçara, açaì, and pejibaye. They have a nutty, artichoke-like flavor and pair well with an endless variety of ingredients. They are easily found in US supermarkets in either cans or jars. In Brazil the most praised kind is the *pupunha*, from yet a fourth kind of palm tree called *pupunheira*, found in the Amazon. It is much larger and meatier then the ones we get in the United States. If you ever go to Brazil, make sure you try a fresh *pupunha*.

SALT COD WITH BACON, ONIONS, EGGS, AND POTATOES

Bacalhau à Bras

Cod fish is often prepared with onions and potatoes in a variety of ways. This version is a favorite of mine. Although all the ingredients are common, the result is captivating. The combination of creamy scrambled eggs with cod, the flavor bursts of bacon and onions, along with the crunch of potatoes, creates a medley new to most American palates. Note that when using salt cod, always allow a bit of planning since you need to soak the cod for at least 24 hours, preferably for 2 to 3 days, in cold water in the refrigerator while changing the water at least 3 times per day. This process allows the cod to be gently poached in milk and cut into tender shreds, which then mix decadently with the savory bacon and eggs and the sweet onions.

MAKES 4 TO 6 SERVINGS

1 ½ pounds salt cod
2 ½ cups milk
2 Idaho potatoes
1 quart canola oil, for frying
2 slices of bacon, finely chopped
3 tablespoons olive oil, and more to drizzle
2 medium onions, thinly sliced
6 large eggs, lightly beaten
3 tablespoons fresh chopped chives
Kosher and normal salt and freshly ground black pepper

DRYING AND DESALTING SALT COD

The best species of cod for salting is the Atlantic cod, gadus morhua. The method of salting cod is rather simple: the fish is split in half lengthwise, cleaned, deboned, and separated by weight. The fish is then covered with salt and kept in plastic containers for 2 to 4 weeks. During this stage it loses almost all the water in their bodies, and the flesh turns from snow white to a light yellow color. The fish is hung in designated rooms with special drying systems that maintain room temperature for another 2 to 4 weeks. Finally, they are sorted by weight and prepared for sale. When using salt cod, it's very important to desalt it properly: use a big plastic container as the volume of water has to be at least 10 times bigger than the weight of the cod. I also like to use a rack or colander so the cod is floating completely in the water.

1   Desalt the cod with the milk as per steps 1–3 on page 19.

2   Cut the potatoes into a julienne cut, using a mandoline. You can also do it by hand but it takes longer. Let the potatoes soak in cold water as you cut them, changing the water at least once. Spread the potatoes onto a baking sheet covered with paper towels to air-dry for 5 minutes, but not much longer as they will start turning brown.

3   Pour the canola oil into a heavy-bottomed pot and heat to 350°F as measured by a deep-fat thermometer. If you don't have a thermometer, drop one potato into the oil—when you hear a sizzling sound and see it turning golden brown, the oil is ready. Fry the potatoes in batches until they are lightly golden brown. Carefully transfer to a plate lined with a double layer of paper towels and sprinkle them with salt. You can prepare the potatoes up to a day in advance, just be sure to keep them in an airtight plastic container.

4   In a large skillet, cook the bacon over medium heat until lightly crisp. Turn the heat to low and add the olive oil and onions and continue to cook, stirring occasionally, until they are soft and translucent, 10 to 15 minutes.

5   Add the shredded cod, then add the eggs all at once to the pan. Mix with a wooden spoon and be careful not to let the eggs dry out. You want them nice and creamy. Add a handful of the string potatoes—they will get mushy when mixed in and that's okay. Season lightly.

6   Pour everything onto a big platter, sprinkle with fresh chives, drizzle with olive oil, and garnish with another handful of string potatoes on top.

COD WITH FINGERLING POTATOES AND ONIONS

Bacalhau à Gomes Sá

This comforting dish is usually made with salt cod and starchy baking potatoes. I chose to use fresh cod and fingerling potatoes, creating a more delicate flavor. Olives, eggs, and fresh herbs help to complete the meal. It's easy to prepare. If you prepare this dish for more than 4 people, do not increase the amount of potatoes—too many will absorb the onion juices, drying out the dish.

MAKES 4 SERVINGS

¾ pound whole fingerling potatoes, peeled
5 tablespoons extra virgin olive oil
2½ cups thinly sliced onion, about 2 large onions
Kosher salt and freshly ground black pepper
2 large eggs, hard-boiled and thinly sliced
¼ cup pitted Kalamata olives, cut in half
1 pound fresh cod
3 tablespoons fresh chopped chives

1   Place the potatoes whole in a large heavy saucepan. Cover them with cold water by at least an inch, add a large pinch of salt, and bring to a boil. Reduce the heat to medium and simmer until the potatoes are fork-tender, 12 to 15 minutes.

2   Drain the potatoes in a colander and spread them out on a plate. When they are cool enough to handle, slice the potatoes into ¼-inch-thick slices. Set aside.

3   Pour 2 tablespoons of the olive oil in a large skillet, add the onions, and cook over low eat, stirring occasionally, until they are tender, sweet, and translucent, 10 to 15 minutes. Resist the temptation to turn the heat to high, otherwise the onions will brown. The slower you cook the onions, the sweeter they get. Transfer to a large bowl.

4   Preheat the oven to 350°F and lightly coat a large shallow baking dish (glass or porcelain) with cooking spray.

5   Add the sliced potatoes to the onions and toss. Season with salt and pepper. Spread them onto the prepared baking dish. Arrange the egg slices and olives on top. Drizzle another 2 tablespoons of the olive oil on top.

6   Season the cod with salt and pepper and place it on top of the potatoes, onions, eggs, and olive mixture. Drizzle 1 tablespoon of olive oil on top of the fish and bake it in the oven until the fish is just cooked, 12 to 15 minutes. The flesh will turn from translucent to opaque white.

7   Remove the baking dish from the oven and garnish with the fresh chives. Spoon the cod onto warm plates and serve hot.

MUSSELS IN COCONUT CREAM SAUCE

Mexilhões com Molho de Côco

Mussels are budget-friendly, easy to prepare, widely available, extremely tasty, and go well with so many flavors. This recipe is just as much about the broth as it is about the mussel. While cooking, the mussels become tender and sweet, and exude their own juices—infusing the sauce with the perfect ocean flavor. It's worth having a piece of bread on the side to catch any leftover sauce. Choose mussels that smell like the ocean, and with tightly shut shells, or shells that shut when tapped, as a sign that they are alive. Discard any mussels that don't open while cooking. Try to buy the mussels the day you'll eat them.

MAKES 4 SERVINGS

3½ to 4 pounds mussels
2 tablespoons dendê oil
¼ cup onion, finely chopped
¼ cup finely chopped yellow bell pepper, about one third of a pepper
¼ cup finely chopped red bell pepper, about one third of a pepper
¼ cup finely chopped green bell pepper, about one third of a pepper
3 cloves garlic, finely minced
1 cup dry white wine
1½ cups coconut milk
kosher salt and freshly ground black pepper
1 plum tomato, peeled, seeded, and diced
2 tablespoons fresh chopped cilantro

1   Rinse and scrub the mussels. Discard any mussel with a cracked shell and remove the bearded hair.

2   In a large pan (enough to handle all the mussels), warm the dendê oil over medium heat. Add the onion and peppers and cook, stirring occasionally, until soft, about 3 minutes. Add the garlic and cook for another minute.

3   Add the mussels and wine. Cover the pan and cook until the mussels open their shells, shaking the pan occasionally, 5 to 8 minutes (be sure not to cook the mussels any longer or they will taste rubbery).

4   Using tongs or a slotted spoon, remove the mussels and place them in a bowl. Cover with a tight lid to keep moist.

5   Bring the remaining sauce to a boil and add the coconut milk. Cook until the sauce reduces and thickens, about 5 minutes. Taste the sauce and season with salt and pepper.

6   Return the mussels and any accumulated juices in the bowl to the pan. Add the tomato, cover, and cook for 2 minutes, just to reheat them.

7   Divide the mussels among 4 plates, spoon the sauce over, and garnish with the cilantro.

SHRIMP STEW IN YUCCA AND COCONUT SAUCE

Bobo de Camarao

Shrimp, dendê oil, coconut milk, and bell peppers makes this recipe one of my favorite flavor combinations of our cuisine. It's all robed in a delicious sauce that relies on a staple vegetable in Brazil: yucca. Most Brazilians cook yucca with coconut milk, then blend it in a food processor or blender. Yucca, however, does not blend well. If you have ever tried mashing potatoes in a food processor, you know the disaster I am referring to. To solve this problem, I injected some French technique. Using white wine, shrimp stock, and mashed yucca instead of blended yucca, results in a stew with better texture and taste. This is a great dish for entertaining or for a fun family meal. Serve it with *farofa* (page 128) or white rice.

1 small yucca, about 11 ounces

3 tablespoons dendê oil

½ cup chopped onion

⅓ cup chopped green bell pepper

⅓ cup chopped yellow bell pepper

2 scallions (white and green parts), chopped

2 stalks celery

4 cloves garlic, finely minced

½ cup white wine

2 cups shrimp stock (see box)

1 cup coconut milk

2 tablespoons tomato paste

1 pound shrimp, uncooked, peeled and deveined

kosher salt and freshly ground black pepper

2 tablespoons unsalted butter

pinch of ground nutmeg

3 plum tomatoes, peeled, seeded, and diced

¼ cup fresh chopped cilantro

1. Follow the instructions on page 32 for preparing and mashing the yucca.

2. Place the dendê oil, onion, peppers, scallions, and celery in a large sauté pan and cook, stirring occasionally, until they are soft and translucent, about 3 minutes.

3. Add the garlic and stir until it gets hot. Add the white wine and reduce by half, 1 to 2 minutes. Add the shrimp stock and coconut milk, then bring the mixture to a boil.

4. Reduce the heat to low and add ½ cup of the mashed yucca and the tomato paste and use a whisk to help dissolve them both into the sauce. The sauce will start to thicken naturally; add up to another ½ cup of the mashed yucca if necessary. Set aside.

5. Season the shrimp with salt and pepper on both sides.

6. In a medium skillet, melt the butter over medium heat. Add the shrimp and cook until they just start to turn orange, about 1 minute each side.

7. Transfer the shrimp to the saucepan. Pour in any shrimp juices that stayed in the skillet and braise the shrimp stew over very low heat, covered, for 5 minutes. Taste the stew and adjust the seasoning with salt, pepper, and nutmeg. Garnish with the tomatoes and cilantro.

BUYING SHRIMP

When it comes to shrimp, both Brazil and the United States are blessed with many varieties. As for size, what some consider medium, others consider large. I recommend that you buy whatever size shrimp you like. Although I prefer to buy shrimp with a fresh-from-the-ocean taste, today's flash-frozen shrimp can be just as good. Just make sure they come in frozen blocks and not individual shrimp, indicating that they haven't been thawed and refrozen, which can affect the quality of the flesh. Because every part of the shrimp is packed with flavor, I always save the shells to make shrimp stock. Making fish stock from scratch is not much fun—you have to gut the fish and remove the gills and eyeballs. So I use shrimp stock for all my fish and shellfish recipes and it works wonderfully while being worlds easier to prepare. See page 112 for a recipe.

SHRIMP WITH HEARTS OF PALM AND TOMATOES

Camarão com Palmito e Tomate

In this recipe, shrimp is paired with hearts of palm, an ingredient that is highly entrenched in the Brazilian vernacular and easy to find fresh all over the country. In the United States, chances are you'll buy it canned, carrying a mild flavor and a trace of acidity from the preserving liquid. To elevate this recipe, consider using langoustines, a tiny lobster-like crustacean with pink shells and fresh hearts of palm. One virtue of shrimp, however, is that they cook in a jiffy. So the key to keeping them moist is by adding them only in the final minutes of cooking. Whenever I eat shellfish, I like a touch of butter, but other than that, this dish is pretty healthy. If you would like to make it more filling, serve it with a side of white rice.

MAKES 4 SERVINGS

2 cups Shrimp Stock (page 112)
1½ pounds large shrimp, peeled and deveined
kosher salt and freshly ground black pepper
4 tablespoons unsalted butter
½ onion, chopped
2 scallions (white and green parts), cut into diagonal small pieces
2 cloves garlic, minced
½ cup dry white wine
1½ cups canned hearts of palm, cut into ½-inch circles on a bias
2 plum tomatoes, peeled, seeded, and chopped
4 tablespoons fresh chopped cilantro

1 Place the shrimp stock in a small saucepan and keep it hot at a low simmer. Season the shrimp with salt and pepper.

2 In a large skillet, melt 2 tablespoons of butter. Add the shrimp and cook until it turns orange and opaque, about 1 minute on each side. Immediately pour the shrimp and juices into a bowl and cover with aluminum foil.

3 Meanwhile, melt 1 tablespoon of butter in the same pan and add the onion and scallions. Cook, scraping all the brown bits left from the shrimp and stirring occasionally, until soft, about 3 minutes. Add the garlic and let it get hot. Add the white wine and reduce by half, about 2 minutes.

4 Add the shrimp stock and bring to a boil, cooking until it starts to thicken, about 5 minutes. Check the seasoning and adjust if necessary. Add the hearts of palm and tomatoes and cook until hot, about 2 minutes.

5 Add the shrimp and any juices that accumulated in the bowl. Cook for 2 to 3 minutes just to reheat them. Add the remaining tablespoon butter, adjust the seasoning if necessary, and garnish with the fresh cilantro.

SHRIMP WITH CHAYOTE

Camarão com Chuchu

Chayote is a mild-flavored, light green vegetable that has been shining for a long time as one of the most basic vegetables in Brazilian home cooking. In Portuguese, it's called *chuchu*, and it grows abundantly just about anywhere it is planted. These days it is becoming easier to find in American supermarkets. This classic dish is delicate and serene, yet bursts with extraordinary flavors mingling from the shrimp and the ultrasucculent texture of the chayote. In my opinion, it needs nothing else, but if you want to add a handful of cherry tomatoes, more for color than for taste, go ahead.

MAKES 4 SERVINGS

1½ cups Shrimp Stock (page 112)
1 pound large shrimp, peeled and
   deveined (13 to 15 shrimp)
kosher salt and freshly ground black pepper
3 chayote (about 8½ ounces each)
4 tablespoons unsalted butter
½ onion, finely chopped
2 cloves garlic, finely minced
a few drops of freshly squeezed lemon juice
4 tablespoons fresh chopped chives

1   Place the shrimp stock in a small saucepan and keep at a low simmer. Season the shrimp with salt and pepper on both sides.

2   Wearing rubber gloves (since chayote is very oily), cut the ends off each chayote and peel the outer skin with a vegetable peeler. Cut the chayote in half vertically from the long side and remove the core using a melon baller or a paring knife. Cut each half into ½-inch–thick slices, then cut each slice into medium pieces on a bias. Place in a bowl, season with salt and pepper, and toss.

3   In a saucepan, melt 2 tablespoons of butter over low heat. Add the chayote and cook, stirring occasionally, without letting it turn brown, about 3 minutes. Add the onion and continue to cook, stirring occasionally, until it gets soft, another 3 minutes. Add the garlic and cook for another minute. Add the stock and simmer everything at low heat until the chayote is soft and tender, 3 to 5 minutes. Don't let the liquid evaporate too much.

4   In a 12-inch skillet, melt the remaining butter, add the shrimp to the pan, and cook until it just starts to turn orange and opaque, about 1 minute per side.

5   Transfer the shrimp and any accumulated juices to the saucepan and simmer everything together at low heat until the flavors start to mingle, 2 to 3 minutes. Make sure not to overcook the shrimp or they will taste rubbery.

6   Add a few drops of lemon juice, season with salt and pepper, and garnish with the chives.

SOLE WITH COCONUT GINGER SAUCE

Linguado e Pimentões com Molho de Coco e Gengibre

Here is a simple and healthy recipe, perfect for a weeknight dinner. Although fish with vegetables is often a dish you'll eat only because it's good for you, this recipe is so flavorful, you might end up craving more. The coconut milk acts not only as an exciting flavor but as a thickening agent, giving body to a creamy sauce while the ginger adds a sharp pungency that complements the texture of the fish and the sweetness of the peppers. Try to dice the bell peppers evenly and very small for a nicer presentation. Both the sauce and the vegetables can be prepared ahead of time. Make sure you buy coconut milk, not coconut juice (the water inside the coconut) or cream of coconut (coconut milk loaded with sugars and emulsifiers).

3 tablespoons olive oil

½ cup chopped red bell pepper

½ cup chopped yellow bell pepper

½ cup chopped green bell pepper

½ cup finely chopped shallots, plus ⅓ cup, chopped

2 cloves garlic, finely minced, plus 2 cloves, chopped

kosher salt and freshly ground black pepper

1 tablespoon fresh chopped thyme

¼ cup fresh chopped ginger

¼ cup dry white wine

1½ cups fish stock

1 cup coconut milk

4 fillets of sole, skinless, about 6 ounces each

1 cup all-purpose flour, for dredging

2 tablespoons unsalted butter

Fresh thyme sprigs, for garnish

1 Heat 2 tablespoons of the olive oil in a large sauté pan over medium heat. Add the peppers and ½ cup shallots and cook, stirring frequently, until soft, 3 to 5 minutes. Add the garlic and cook for another minute. Season with salt and pepper and add the thyme. Keep warm but off the heat.

2 To make the sauce, place the remaining olive oil and shallots in a medium saucepan and cook over medium heat, stirring often, until soft and translucent, about 5 minutes. Add the ginger and garlic and continue cooking and stirring for another 2 minutes. Pour in the white wine and reduce by 80 percent.

3 Add the fish stock and bring to a boil. Add the coconut milk and stir well, and cook over low heat until the sauce reaches a proper consistency. To test, place 1 tablespoon of sauce on a plate; it should just hold its shape. If the sauce is too runny, reduce a little longer and if it's too thick, add a little bit more coconut milk or wine. Pass the sauce through a fine sieve and into another saucepan. Discard the solids. Season with salt and pepper and keep warm.

4 Meanwhile, prepare the sole. Lay the fillets on a baking sheet and gently pat them dry with a paper towel. Season with salt and pepper on both sides. Dredge the fish in flour on both sides and shake off the excess.

5 In a large skillet, melt the butter over medium heat and swirl it to cover the whole pan. Gently lay the fish in the pan; they should sizzle lightly. Try not to move the fish around so that it creates a golden crust on each side. Cook until the fillets are golden brown on both sides, 2 to 3 minutes per side. Be careful when turning the fish over; use a metal spatula to avoid cracking the crust. Transfer the fish to warm plates or a platter.

6 Spread a thin layer of the warm peppers on top of the fish. Spoon the sauce around the fish and garnish with a sprig of thyme.

CHOOSING SOLE

Most of the fish in the sole family that we buy today is either gray sole (second choice), lemon sole (third choice), or flounder (last choice). These fish are less fatty than the Dover sole, which is harder to find and more expensive, but it is my first choice and favorite of all soles. However, the flavor and body of the coconut-ginger sauce is a delicious accompaniement to any sole, and all sole varieties have a wonderful flavor. You can also use turbot or tilapia.

FISH PURÉE WITH COCONUT MILK

Vatapá

Vatapá is a classic dish from Brazil's Bahia region. It is a purée of fish, bread, coconut milk, shrimp stock, cashews, peanuts, onions, tomatoes, dendê oil, ginger, and dried shrimp. The dried shrimp found in the United States carries more shell than meat, and by the time it's ground it becomes very gritty. So I make a version without it and it is just as delicious. In Brazil, *vatapá* is mostly used as a spread or a filling for *acarajé* (I use it as a dip on page 30). Here, I use it as a bed for fresh shrimp, but you can also spread it over flatbread and top it with shrimp and tomato (see page 28). *Vatapá* can be prepared with any other white fish such as snapper, grouper, or sea bass instead of halibut. Also try a shrimp-based *vatapá*.

(I use it as a dip on page 30) ... (see page 28)

MAKES 6 TO 8 SERVINGS

½ cup unsalted peanuts, roasted
½ cup unsalted cashews, roasted
2 cups shrimp stock
1 pound halibut
kosher salt and freshly ground black pepper
4 tablespoons tomato paste
2 slices white bread with crusts removed, diced
1¾ cups coconut milk
3 tablespoons dendê oil
½ onion, diced
1 scallion (white and green parts), chopped
3 cloves garlic, finely minced
1 teaspoon peeled and finely grated fresh ginger, or ¼ teaspoon ground
4 plum tomatoes, peeled, seeded, and diced
1 tablespoon fresh lemon juice
⅛ teaspoon turmeric
⅛ teaspoon smoked Spanish paprika

1½ pounds medium shrimp, peeled and deveined
2 tablespoons dendê oil
½ cup fresh chopped cilantro, for garnish

1   In the bowl of a food processor, process the peanuts and cashews until they are finely ground, but not quite a paste. Transfer to a bowl and set aside.

2   Bring the shrimp stock to a simmer and keep the heat low. Season the fish with salt and pepper on both sides. Carefully immerse the fish in the simmering stock and poach until the fish is cooked through, 3 to 5 minutes. Do not let the liquid boil. Transfer the fish to a plate and cover with aluminum foil.

3   Add the tomato paste to the stock and whisk until it is completely dissolved. Turn off the heat.

4   In a medium bowl, soak the bread in the coconut milk until it becomes moist and soft, about 5 minutes. Set aside.

5   Pour the 3 tablespoons of dendê oil in a large saucepan and cook the onion and scallion over medium heat, stirring occasionally, until soft, 3 to 4 minutes. Add the garlic and ginger and cook for another minute.

6   Place the fish in the bowl of a food processor. Add the bread with all of the coconut milk. Process until you have a coarse fish purée, about 2 minutes. Carefully pour the fish purée into the saucepan, scraping the sides of the bowl with a spatula to get it all out.

7   Add the ground nuts and tomatoes and stir everything well with a wooden spoon. Add the shrimp stock, lemon juice, turmeric, and paprika and season with salt and pepper.

Simmer for 5 to 10 minutes, partially covered. Keep warm, or store the *vatapá* in an airtight plastic container for up to 2 days in the refrigerator.

8   Season the shrimp with salt and pepper on both sides.

9   Pour the 2 tablespoons of dendê oil in a large skillet over medium heat. Add the shrimp, and cook until they just turn orange, 30 seconds to 1 minute on each side.

10   To serve, place a spoonful of *vatapá* in a bowl and top with shrimp. Pour any of the dende oil remaining in the pan over the shrimp. Garnish with the fresh cilantro.

FISH IN SPICED HONEY

Filet de Peixe ao Mel Picante

My friends Patty Pulliam and Sergey Boyce are beekeepers in Connecticut, and from them I learned that honey absorbs a wide variety of flavors when infused with certain ingredients. After a lesson on cooking with honey and a freshly harvested golden jar in my hands, I was inspired to add some Brazilian spices. After a few hours of marinating, you'll be rewarded with a sweet crusted fish that is full of flavor with a delicate snow white inside (you can try this with chicken, too). Make sure to save some spiced honey to baste the fish—but at the end of the cooking process, otherwise the honey might caramelize and harden in the pan.

MAKES 4 SERVINGS

¾ cup sherry vinegar
¼ cup honey
1 tablespoon soy sauce
2 tablespoons fresh orange juice
1 cinnamon stick
½ teaspoon fennel seeds
4 cardamom pods
1 ounce fresh ginger, peeled and finely chopped

four 6-ounce halibut fillets, center cut, skinless
kosher salt and freshly ground black pepper
2 tablespoons extra virgin olive oil

1 Place the first 8 ingredients in a medium saucepan and bring to a boil. Reduce the heat to low and simmer until the liquid reduces to a light syrupy consistency, 4 to 6 minutes. Remove from the heat and let cool completely in the pan. You'll have ½ to ¾ cup of reduced honey, which you can refrigerate in an airtight plastic container for up to 5 days.

2 Place the halibut fillets in a large ziplock bag and pour all of the honey reduction (save 2 to 3 tablespoons) with all of the spices into the bag. Rub the reduction around the fish until the fillets are evenly coated. Remove the air from the plastic bag and seal well. Place in the refrigerator for 3 to 5 hours.

3 Remove the fish from the refrigerator at least 20 minutes before cooking. Preheat the oven to 375°F.

4 Remove the fish from the honey reduction and wipe off any remaining fennel seeds but do not pat dry as you want the sugar in the honey to glaze the fish. Season with salt and pepper.

5 Heat the olive oil in a large ovenproof skillet over medium to high heat. Add the fish and cook until lightly golden brown, 2 to 3 minutes per side. Pour the reserved reduction over the fish and transfer the pan to the oven. Bake until the fish is cooked through, about 5 minutes. Transfer the fish to 4 dinner plates and spoon any remaining reduction on top.

STRIPED BASS WITH CASHEW SOY SAUCE

Peixe com Molho de Manteiga e Castanhas

Inspired by both Asian and Brazilian cuisines, this recipe is perfect for a weeknight dinner. Soy sauce makes a fine sauce here, thinned with nutty browned butter, lemon juice, shallot, and a dash of sugar. But that's just the beginning. You add peanuts, cashews, and chives before serving. Ultimately, you'll be rewarded with a mahogany-colored, intensely flavored, and crunchy sauce. Feel free to use this sauce with other fish as well, such as halibut, monkfish, salmon, and scallops. Just be sure to adapt the cooking time for each fish.

MAKES 4 SERVINGS

14 tablespoons unsalted butter (1¾ sticks)
3 tablespoons fresh lemon juice
2 tablespoons soy sauce
1 shallot, finely minced
⅛ teaspoon sugar
four 5-ounce striped bass fillets, skin-on
kosher salt and freshly ground black pepper
⅓ cup cashews, roasted and coarsely chopped
⅓ cup peanuts, roasted and coarsely chopped
2 tablespoons fresh chopped chives

1 In a medium saucepan over low heat, melt 12 tablespoons of butter until it develops a light golden brown color. Be careful not to let it burn. Add the lemon juice, soy sauce, shallot, and sugar. Whisk the sauce, then remove the pan from the heat, but keep it in a warm spot on the stove.

2 Make two or three small diagonal cuts on the skin of the fish without piercing the flesh. Season with salt and pepper on both sides.

3 In a large nonstick skillet over medium heat, melt the remaining 2 tablespoons butter and add the fish skin side down. Depending on the thickness of the fish, it might curve so use a flat metal spatula to press the skin down against the skillet, making sure it becomes crispy. Cook until the fish turns opaque, about 2 minutes on each side.

4 Reheat the sauce gently over low heat and whisk vigorously to blend it smooth. Add the cashews, peanuts, and chives.

5 To serve, arrange the fish on 4 warm plates and spoon the sauce on top.

BAKED SHELLFISH FRITTATA

Torta Capixaba

When you see the word *capixaba*, you can be sure that whatever is being served originates from the state of Espirito Santo, located above the state of Rio de Janeiro, along Brazil's southeastern coast. Traditional Torta Capixaba is a giant mixture of fish and shellfish of all types in a frittata with additional whipped egg whites on top; everything is baked in an old style clay baking dish. It certainly served as my template for this short-order frittata, which is definitely a more approachable dish than the original. Use any combination of shellfish you like and keep the quantities I've provided as your guidelines. You can use clams, lobster, mussels, calamari, or oysters. This recipe should help you cook the shellfish to perfection: First, they're given a quick toss on the stovetop, then they are mixed with lightly beaten eggs and poured into a baking dish (you can use individual ramekins too), and baked in the oven until the eggs are just set. As a matter of taste, eggs must not be overcooked, so be as careful when baking the frittata as you are when cooking the shellfish, and you'll have a stunning dinner at the table.

MAKES 4 SERVINGS

2 tablespoons olive oil

1 medium onion, thinly sliced

1 scallion (white and green parts), thinly sliced on a bias

3 cloves garlic, finely minced

½ pound shrimp, shelled

¼ pound bay scallops

kosher salt and freshly ground black pepper

½ pound jumbo lump crabmeat

2 plum tomatoes, peeled, seeded, and thinly sliced

2 tablespoons green olives, pitted, and halved (optional)

4 large eggs

2 tablespoons fresh chopped parsley

9-inch round baking dish

1   Preheat the oven to 350°F. Grease a round baking dish with cooking spray.

2   Pour the olive oil in a large sauté pan, add the onion and scallion, and cook over medium heat, stirring occasionally, until soft, about 3 minutes. Be careful not to let them brown. Add the garlic and cook for another minute.

3   Season the shrimp and bay scallops with kosher salt on all sides. Add them to the pan, reduce the heat to low, and cook until they start to turn opaque, about 2 minutes. Add the crab, tomatoes, and green olives, if using, and stir everything together. Season with salt and pepper and transfer to a bowl.

4   In a separate medium bowl, break the eggs and season with salt and pepper. Lightly whisk the eggs and pour them into the shellfish mixture. Add the parsley and fold everything together with a rubber spatula.

5   Pour the mixture into the prepared baking dish and bake in the oven until the eggs are just set, 20 to 30 minutes. Do not overcook or the eggs will dry out.

6   To serve, remove the dish from the oven and rush it to the table. Divide it among warm dinner plates and enjoy.

SALMON WITH CAIPIRINHA RISOTTO

Salmon com Risotto de Caipirinha

I like to incorporate the flavors of a Caipirinha (page 14) into other dishes, both sweet and savory. I always think of risotto as being a great flavor receptor, so I decided to try a caipirinha risotto. I thought of the classic Italian penne à la vodka where the pasta receives a boost of alcohol. This is an excellent rice dish with many kinds of fish—salmon is my favorite, but scallops, halibut, skate, and shrimp all work splendidly with the sharp flavors of lime and cachaça in this warm and creamy risotto. I emphasize the word creamy—all too often I find risottos are served thick, dried, and pasty. Add a few tablespoons of broth just before serving to ensure a creamy state. This is a glamorous and different dish to make for an entertaining, yet not overly complicated, weeknight dinner.

4½ cups Shrimp Stock (page 112)

5 tablespoons unsalted butter

4 tablespoons extra virgin olive oil, plus extra for drizzling

½ medium onion, finely diced

1 cup Arborio rice

four 4-ounce salmon fillets, skinless

kosher salt and freshly ground black pepper

grated zest of 1 lime

4 teaspoons fresh lime juice

⅓ cup cachaça

2 tablespoons fresh chopped dill, plus a few
   sprigs for garnish

1 tablespoon crème fraîche

1   In a large saucepan, bring the stock to a boil over high heat. Reduce the heat to low and keep the stock at a slow, steady simmer.

2   Melt 2 tablespoons of the butter and 2 tablespoons of the olive oil in a large Dutch oven or sauté pan over medium heat. Add the onion and cook, stirring often, until soft and translucent, about 5 minutes. Add the rice and cook while still stirring, until all the grains are coated with the onion and butter and the rice looks shiny, about 3 minutes.

3   Add 1 large ladle of simmering stock at a time. Cook, stirring often, until the liquid is absorbed by the rice. Add another ladle, and keep cooking and stirring. Continue adding ladles of stock only when the previous one has been completely absorbed. Keep the heat low because you'll prepare the salmon while the risotto is cooking.

4   Season the salmon fillets on both sides with salt and pepper.

5   In a large skillet over medium heat, add the remaining 2 tablespoons of olive oil. Place the salmon top side down and cook for about 2 minutes on each side (if you like your salmon well done, cook it a little longer). Try to coordinate the cooking of the salmon with the risotto; the rice should be just a few minutes from being done by the time the fillets are finished.

6   The rice should be al dente and almost all of the liquid absorbed within 15 minutes of starting. Remove it from the heat and season with salt and pepper. Add the lime zest, lime juice, cachaça, and dill. Mix everything well with a wooden spoon.

7   Add the remaining 3 tablespoons of butter and the crème fraîche. Add another tablespoon or so of stock if the risotto has absorbed all of its liquid.

8   Spoon the risotto into warm bowls. Place the salmon on top and garnish with a sprig of dill and a drizzle of olive oil.

RISOTTO COOKING TIP

You've probably heard this many times before, but when making risotto, try to keep a slight crunchiness to the grain, cooking it al dente. Risotto can be prepared ahead of time, despite what some may tell you: Remove it from the stove after the second or third addition of liquid, spread it onto a flat sheet pan to cool it down. Resume cooking when you are ready to cook the fish.

TILAPIA WITH AÇAÍ SAUCE

Peixe no Molho de Açaí

MAKES 4 SERVINGS

1 tablespoon unsalted butter

1 medium shallot, minced

1 bay leaf

⅓ cup frozen açaí pulp, thawed (about 3 ounces)

⅓ cup crème de cassis

2 tablespoons raspberry jam

½ cup Shrimp Stock (page 112)

kosher salt and freshly ground black pepper

¼ cup heavy cream

four 6-ounce tilapia fillets, skinless

½ cup all-purpose flour

2 tablespoons olive oil

¼ cup fresh chopped mint leaves, for garnish

Açaí, the little crown jewel berry from the Amazon, is taking America by storm due to its high nutritional content. It can be a truly interesting ingredient if bought in frozen pulps, and it can be prepared in many ways, both sweet or savory, just like a berry. Its taste is so strong—a blend of red wine and chocolate—that the fruit is often matched with other berries to lighten it up a little. In this recipe, *açaí* adds a depth of flavor to a sauce that complements a simply cooked fish. Grouper, monkfish, halibut, or even swordfish, all work well with the sweet taste of *açaí*, but the humble tilapia, lightly crisped in flour and olive oil, is my favorite.

1   Melt the butter in a medium saucepan over medium heat. Add the shallot and cook, stirring frequently, until soft, 2 to 3 minutes.

2   Add the bay leaf, açaí, cassis, raspberry jam, and shrimp stock. Bring everything to a boil, then reduce the heat to low and cook at a quiet simmer, until the sauce starts to get thick and syrupy, about 10 minutes. Season lightly with salt and pepper.

3   Strain the sauce through a fine sieve into a small saucepan. Add the heavy cream and bring to a simmer again, until blended, about 2 minutes. The sauce can be refrigerated in an airtight container for up to 2 days.

4   Season the fish on both sides with salt and pepper. Dredge the fish in the flour on both sides and shake off the excess.

5   Pour the olive oil in a large nonstick pan and cook the fish over medium heat until it's lightly golden brown, 2 to 3 minutes per side. Transfer the fish to a plate lined with paper towels to absorb the excess oil.

6   Serve the fish on a warm plate and spoon the sauce on top and around. Garnish with the mint.

CHICKEN FEIJOADA

Feijoada de Galinha

The national dish of Brazil, *feijoada* is a crowd pleaser. This recipe is a faster version, but it certainly retains all the warmth of the slow-simmered original. I developed this recipe with a large party in mind, but I have also been using it for weeknight dinners by simply using one chicken and halving the amount of beans. My favorite way to vary this recipe is to use different types of beans. I encourage you to follow suit, but be advised that different types and different brands of beans, will vary the cooking time substantially. Different bean varieties (as long as they are dried beans) such as red, pinto, kidney, and white all blend splendidly in this *feijoada*. While you can't get too fancy with a *feijoada*, you also can't get closer to our cuisine's roots. And if you crave the taste of Brazil like I do, eat it again the next day because it re-heats fantastically. Serve it with white rice or *farofa* (page 128).

MAKES 8 TO 10 SERVINGS

1 pound black beans from a bag, rinsed and picked through, about 2¾ cups

2½ to 3 quarts cold water, enough to cover the beans by 2 inches

2 chickens, 3½ to 4 pounds each with skin, cut up into 6 pieces each

kosher salt and freshly ground black pepper

4 tablespoons canola oil

½ cup white wine

1 onion, chopped

2 stalks celery, finely chopped

4 scallions (green and white parts), finely chopped

⅔ cup finely chopped green bell pepper

5 cloves garlic, minced

3 bay leaves

freshly ground nutmeg

cayenne pepper to taste

2 tablespoons fresh chopped parsley

1 Place the beans in a very large pot, and cover them with the cold water. Cover the pan and bring the water to a boil over high heat. Bring the heat down to medium-high and cook the beans, covered, until they are just cooked but not too mushy, 1 to 1½ hours. At this point the liquid will still look thin and clear. Keep the beans in the liquid and set them aside. This step can be completed up to two days ahead of time; just keep the beans and the liquid in an airtight plastic container in the refrigerator.

2 While the beans are cooking, prepare the chicken. Pat the chicken pieces dry with paper towels and season with salt and pepper on both sides.

3 Pour 2 tablespoons of the canola oil in a large sauté pan and cook the chicken, in batches, over medium heat until it is golden brown, about 4 minutes per side. Transfer to a bowl and cover with aluminum foil, making sure steam cannot escape.

4 Use the white wine to deglaze the pan by scraping the pan with a wooden spoon, making sure all the brown bits and jus gets transferred to the liquid. Boil until the liquid is well infused with flavor, then strain it into a bowl. Set aside.

5 Pour the remaining 2 tablespoons of canola oil into a large Dutch oven and cook the onion, celery, scallions, and bell pepper over medium heat, stirring, until soft, about 3 minutes. Add the garlic and cook another minute. Add the chicken and all the juice that might have accumulated in the bowl. Add the reserved beans and all their liquid, and the strained deglazing liquid. The chicken should be covered almost entirely with the beans, vegetables, and liquid.

6 Add the bay leaves and simmer on very low heat with the pan uncovered so that the

liquid has a chance to reduce and thicken. Cook until the chicken meat is tender and sliding off the bone, 1 to 1½ hours.

7 Before finishing, slightly tilt the pan and scoop out any chicken fat. The black bean sauce should be glossy and earthy. Season with salt, pepper, nutmeg, and cayenne. Top with the fresh parsley.

8 To serve, place a piece of chicken in a bowl over the starch of your choice, and top with a ladle of the bean sauce.

CHICKEN AND PLANTAIN MOQUECA

Moqueca de Galinha e Banana-da-Terra

This is a tame version of the traditional seafood *moqueca*. The plantain brings a soft sweetness and plenty of starch to the stew. Some recipes call for green plantains, which are treated like a potato, but true Brazilians prefer to eat their plantains ripe or semiripe, when the fruit has a fuller balance of sweetness and starch and carries more juice.

This is a straightforward braising dish that takes a bit longer than the fish version (about 1½ hours), but when you taste the dynamic combination of chicken and plantain, you will experience comforting flavors and textures that make this *moqueca* worth the wait.

MAKES 4 TO 6 SERVINGS

1 whole chicken (about 3½ pounds), with skin, cut into 8 pieces

kosher salt and freshly ground black pepper

4 tablespoons dendê oil

1 medium onion, thinly sliced

2 scallions (white and green parts), sliced on the diagonal

½ green bell pepper, thinly sliced

½ cup white wine

4 cloves garlic, finely minced

1 small piece of fresh ginger, peeled and finely grated

3 cups chicken stock

1½ cups coconut milk

3 tablespoons tomato paste

2 bay leaves

1 pound ripe plantains (look for yellow and black-speckled skin)

3 plum tomatoes, peeled, seeded, and sliced

4 tablespoons fresh chopped cilantro

1   Place the chicken pieces in a medium bowl. Season with salt and pepper and 2 tablespoons of the dendê oil. Rub the chicken all over with the oil making sure it is well distributed. Cover the bowl with plastic wrap and marinate at room temperature for 15 to 30 minutes.

2   Pour the remaining dendê oil into a large Dutch oven and swirl around so the entire bottom is covered. Add the chicken pieces, skin side down, and brown them lightly, over medium heat, for 3 minutes per side.

3   Using a pair of tongs, transfer the chicken pieces to a clean bowl and cover with aluminum foil, making sure no steam can escape.

4   Add the onion, scallions, and bell pepper to the pan and cook them in the leftover dendê oil, stirring often, until soft, about 4 minutes. Add the white wine and reduce by half, while using a wooden spoon to scrape the brown bits that stayed in the pan. Add the garlic and ginger and cook, stirring, for another minute. Add the chicken stock, coconut milk, tomato paste, and bay leaves and bring to a boil.

5   Reduce the heat to the lowest setting. Add the chicken and any remaining juices that accumulated in the bowl. Season lightly with salt and pepper. Simmer, covered, until the chicken starts to get tender, about 1 hour.

6   Meanwhile, trim the ends off the plantains and cut 3 to 4 vertical slits in the skin, making sure not to cut deep into the fruit. Peel and cut the plantains into 1-inch chunks.

7   Add the plantains to the *moqueca* after it has been simmering for an hour. Cover and continue to simmer until the plantains become soft but not mushy, 10 to 15 minutes. If the liquid seems too runny, uncover the pan and continue to simmer, allowing the steam to evaporate and thicken the stew. Season with salt and pepper.

8   Just a few minutes before serving, add the tomatoes. Garnish with the fresh cilantro and serve over white rice or *farofa* (page 128).

BRAZILIAN CHICKEN EMPANADA

Empadao de Frango

This is a delicious savory tart of shredded chicken encased in a buttery and flaky crust. With the addition of corn, peas, tomatoes, and hearts of palm, it is a great meal in itself with a green salad on the side. This recipe yields two tarts from just one chicken. Once assembled the tarts can be stored unbaked in the refrigerator (covered loosely with plastic wrap) for up to 3 days or frozen for up to a month. It's easy to add other vegetables or types of meat to the filling. Shredded duck or turkey make excellent variations.

1   Place the flour and salt in a bowl and set aside. In the bowl of an electric mixer fitted with the paddle attachment, beat the butter at medium speed until creamy. Add the eggs and milk. Add the flour and salt and turn the speed to low. Depending on the humidity, you might need up to 3 tablespoons of water to help the dough form into a ball.

2   Place the ball of dough onto a floured surface and press into a flat disk. Wrap in plastic wrap and refrigerate for at least 30 minutes.

3   Meanwhile, prepare the filling. In a medium saucepan, bring the stock to a boil over high heat. Reduce the heat to low and add the tomato paste, whisking well to dissolve.

MAKES 4 TO 6 SERVINGS

FOR THE DOUGH

3 ⅓ cups all-purpose flour, sifted
4 teaspoons salt
3 sticks unsalted butter, cold
2 whole eggs
¼ cup whole milk

FOR THE FILLING

5 cups chicken stock
2 tablespoons tomato paste
8 tablespoons (1 stick) unsalted butter
1 cup all-purpose flour
kosher salt and freshly ground black pepper
freshly ground nutmeg
2 tablespoons extra virgin olive oil
1 large onion, chopped
6 cloves garlic, minced
1¼ cups frozen peas, thawed
1¼ cups frozen corn kernels, thawed
1 cup diced hearts of palm
3 plum tomatoes, peeled, seeded, and diced
4½ cups shredded cooked chicken, packed tight (light and
   dark meat from 1 whole cooked 1½-pound chicken)
½ cup fresh chopped chives

1 beaten egg for the egg wash
two 8-inch round porcelain pie pans

4   Melt the butter in a different saucepan over low heat. Add the flour all at once and stir to make a roux, about 2 minutes. Add the stock and whisk constantly, over medium heat, until it thickens. Season with salt and pepper and nutmeg and set aside.

5   Warm the olive oil in a large saucepan over low heat. Add the onion and cook, stirring occasionally, until soft and translucent, about 2 minutes. Add the garlic and cook for another minute. Add the peas, corn, hearts of palm, and tomatoes, stirring constantly. Add the chicken and cook for 5 minutes. Season with salt, pepper, and nutmeg. Transfer to a large bowl.

6   Pour the creamy chicken stock into the bowl and mix well. Add the chives and adjust the seasoning. Spread the filling onto a baking sheet and let cool completely before assembling. Remove the dough from the refrigerator at least 20 minutes before rolling.

7   Cut the dough into four pieces. On a lightly floured surface, roll the dough into circles about 1/16 inch thick. Unroll the dough onto the tart mold and up the sides, leaving some extra dough hanging on the edges. Spread half of the filling inside the mold. Using a pastry brush dipped in water, lightly moisten the edges of the bottom crust.

8   Repeat the rolling process with another round of dough and center it over the chicken filling. Fold a bit of extra top dough onto the mold. Press the top crust against the bottom crust in an attractive way with your fingers, then trim the overhang from both crusts. Using a paring knife, cut an X in the center of the crust to vent while baking.

9   Repeat steps 7 through 9 with the second pie. Place the *empadão* in the refrigerator for at least 1 hour before baking. At this point

you can cover it with plastic wrap and store it in the refrigerator for up to 3 days or freeze it for up to 3 months.

10   Preheat the oven to 350°F. Place the *empadão* on a sheet pan and bake on the center rack of the oven until the top looks lightly brown, 30 to 40 minutes.

11   Remove from the oven, brush the top crust with the egg wash and return to the oven until the crust is golden brown, 10 to 15 minutes.

12   Transfer the *empadão* to a rack and let it rest for 20 minutes before serving. Unlike a chicken pot pie which is served bubbling out of the oven, the *empadão* (or other sizes of *empada*) should never be served too hot. To best enjoy it, serve it warm.

CHICKEN, SHRIMP, PEANUT, AND CASHEW STEW

Xim Xim de Galinha

This stew is about simple ingredients with an exotic result. The favorite Bahian combination of chicken and shrimp comes together in a creamy sauce. The nuts serve as the perfect binding agents for the coconut milk and chicken stock, but they have to be finely ground—if they are too coarse, they just won't do the work. On the other hand, you have to be careful not to turn the nuts into a paste. The recipe can be prepared up to 2 days ahead of time and it reheats extremely well. If you prefer to make it ahead of time, it's best to hold the shrimp and add them to the pan 5 minutes before serving. I like to serve this dish by itself, but if you would like a starch to go with it, white rice or *farofa* (page 128) would be nice.

MAKES 6 TO 8 SERVINGS

1 whole chicken (3 to 4 pounds), cut into 8 pieces with the skin on

3 cloves garlic, coarsely chopped

3 tablespoons fresh lime juice

½ pound medium shrimp, peeled and deveined, about 20 shrimp

4 tablespoons dendê oil

kosher salt and freshly ground black pepper

½ cup unsalted peanuts, roasted

½ cup unsalted cashews, roasted

4 tablespoons extra virgin olive oil

1 medium onion, finely chopped

2 scallions (white and green parts), chopped

4 plum tomatoes, peeled, seeded, and diced

1 tablespoon tomato paste

1½ cups coconut milk

1½ cups chicken stock

¼ teaspoon turmeric

⅛ teaspoon paprika

½ cup fresh chopped cilantro

1 Place the chicken pieces in a medium bowl and add the garlic and lime juice. Rub the chicken all over with the juice, making sure it is well distributed. Cover the bowl with plastic wrap and marinate at room temperature for 15 to 30 minutes.

2 In another bowl, place the shrimp and 2 tablespoons of the dendê oil. Cover the bowl with plastic wrap and marinate for 15 minutes at room temperature. (If you are making the dish ahead of time, save the shrimp and marinade.)

3 Meanwhile, in the bowl of a food processor, process the peanuts and cashews until they are finely ground, but don't become a paste. Transfer to a bowl and set aside.

4 Remove the chicken from the marinade and wipe off any remaining garlic. Lightly pat the chicken dry with a paper towel and season with salt and pepper on both sides.

5 Pour 2 tablespoons of the olive oil in a large sauté pan and cook the chicken pieces over medium heat, until they are lightly browned, about 3 minutes on each side. You don't want the chicken to cook completely, as it will finish during braising. If necessary, cook it in batches, and as you remove the chicken pieces, place them on a plate and cover them with foil to keep them warm.

6 Add the remaining 2 tablespoons of olive oil and cook the onion and scallions, stirring occasionally and scraping the brown bits off the bottom of the pan, until the onion is soft, about 2 minutes. Add the tomatoes, tomato paste, and ground nuts and cook, stirring to blend well, about 1 minute. Add the coconut milk, chicken stock, turmeric, and paprika, and let the sauce come to a simmer.

7 Lower the heat to its lowest setting, then add the chicken pieces and all the juices that have accumulated in the bowl. Cover and simmer until the chicken is cooked through, although it should remain tender and moist, 25 to 30 minutes. (Reserve the stew at this point if you want to serve it at a later date. Store it in an airtight plastic container in the refrigerator for up to 2 days.)

8 Meanwhile, remove the shrimp from the bowl and pat them dry. Season with salt and pepper on both sides.

9 In a medium skillet, heat the remaining dendê oil and cook the shrimp until they start to turn orange, about 1 minute per side.

10 Pour the shrimp and any remaining dendê oil from the pan right into the chicken stew, cover, and cook so the shrimp has a chance to braise with the chicken, 3 to 4 minutes. At this point the mixture should look orange and the nuts will have thickened the stew but also made it slightly gritty. You want it to be just a little pasty from the nuts. If the stew is too thick, add another tablespoon or so of chicken stock. Adjust the seasoning with salt and pepper. Garnish with the cilantro.

CUTTING CHICKEN

When cutting a chicken, aim for 2 wings, 2 breasts, 2 drumsticks, and 2 thighs. If that takes up a lot of space in the pan, requiring you to use two skillets, you can also cut the chicken into 6 pieces, leaving the thigh and drum attached and cutting them apart only at the braising stage. You can also buy the chicken precut from the market.

SLOW-ROASTED DUCK BREAST WITH CUPUAÇU SAUCE

Peito de Pato Assado com Molho de Cupuaçú

Duck pairs well with flavors from all over the world, and cooking duck with a sweet fruit sauce is classic. I decided to experiment with fruits for a small duck breast, one that would cook quickly for a weeknight dinner, and I thought of cupuaçú (see Glossary on page 170) because I love its banana-like consistency, and its tangy qualities fit perfectly with the outer layer of fat and the sweetness of the duck meat. Serve with a green vegetable such as Collard Greens (page 123) or broccoli.

MAKES 2 SERVINGS

1 duck breast, skin on (about 1 pound)
kosher salt and freshly ground black pepper

FOR THE SAUCE
1 tablespoon olive oil
2 large shallots, coarsely chopped
¾ cup chicken stock
⅔ cup cupuaçú pulp, thawed
2 tablespoons orange marmalade
1 tablespoon honey
3 tablespoons unsalted butter, cold, and cubed

1. Remove the duck breast from the refrigerator about 1 hour before cooking. Preheat the oven to 275°F.

2. Trim the excess fat from the duck, leaving a layer on one side. Trim any silver skin and remove the small tender from the duck breast to allow even cooking. Score the fat side with 4 to 5 cuts in a crosshatch pattern, being careful not to pierce the meat. Season both sides with salt and pepper—lightly on the flesh side and a bit heavier on the fat.

3. Place the duck, fat side down, in a medium ovenproof skillet over high heat. The pan should sizzle on contact with the duck. Cook until browned, about 2 minutes. Spoon any rendered fat into a bowl. Turn the duck over and quickly sear the flesh, about 1 minute.

4. Immediately transfer the skillet to the oven and slow-roast the duck until the meat is cooked rare to medium rare all the way through, 12 to 14 minutes.

5. Meanwhile, prepare the sauce. Pour the olive oil into a medium saucepan and cook the shallots over medium heat until soft and translucent, about 2 minutes. Add the chicken stock, cupuaçú pulp, orange marmalade, and honey and simmer over medium to low heat until the sauce reaches a syrupy consistency, about 5 minutes.

6. Strain the sauce through a fine sieve into another saucepan. You will have about 1 cup. Discard the solids. Bring the sauce back to a simmer over very low heat.

7. Add the cold butter and whisk it into the sauce, about 2 minutes. Once the butter is added to the sauce, don't boil it or it will curdle. Keep the heat very low and swirl the pan often. Season with salt and pepper.

8. Remove the duck from the oven and let it rest for at least 5 minutes. Slice on a bias and serve with some sauce spooned on top.

COOKING DUCK

Some people are afraid of cooking duck at home, especially when it comes to the breast. The meat has a tendency to become chewy if served rare, which is how we all learn duck needs to be served. Cooked correctly though, duck breast is quite simple to prepare. The key to perfection is to sauté the breast, skin side down, until it's nicely browned, then roast it slowly over a low temperature so that the fat has time to render and the meat is cooked equally rare as opposed to seared on the edges and red in the center.

The three most common breeds of duck are Pekin, Muscovy, and Mallard. The Pekin (not to be confused with Peking, which is a style of cooking duck) is originally from China, but is being farmed in Long Island, New York, and Sonoma Bay, California. It's probably the most common variety, found in supermarkets all over the country. Each Pekin duck weighs 4 to 5 pounds, feeding two people. The Muscovy duck weighs about 7 to 8 pounds and has a redder meat, is very lean, and has a more pronounced flavor. The male Muscovy duck produces some of the best foie gras. With less fat and less of an oily taste, the Mallard duck is wilder than the other two varieties, producing a gamey flavor. Any of the breeds can be used in this recipe.

CHICKEN BRAISED WITH CARAMELIZED ONIONS

Galinha Moreninha

Lourdes Paixao is a wonderful grandmotherly figure who cooks by memory the food of her home in Minas Gerais, where most of the cuisine is hearty and earthy. She is the kind of cook who doesn't use a cutting board—she holds vegetables with one hand and cuts them with a small knife in the other over a plastic bowl. She cooks under any circumstances, with any equipment, on any stove, and in any kitchen. One of her best dishes is this chicken dish, a cross between French onion soup and osso buco. The onions are caramelized and the legs are slowly braised until the meat falls apart. The result is a velvety chicken stew full of flavor.

1. Season the chicken pieces with salt and pepper.

2. Heat the olive oil in a large skillet over medium-high heat. Add the chicken pieces skin side down and cook until they are golden brown, about 4 minutes per side. Transfer to a bowl and cover with aluminum foil.

3. Turn the heat to low and add the onions. Cook, stirring frequently, until they caramelize, 25 to 30 minutes. If you see onions burning on the sides, add a tablespoon of water.

MAKES 4 TO 6 SERVINGS

4 whole chicken legs, cut into legs and thighs
kosher salt and freshly ground black pepper
2 tablespoons olive oil
2 large onions, finely sliced
3 cloves garlic, sliced
½ cup Madeira wine
3 cups veal stock
2 plum tomatoes, peeled, seeded, and chopped
2 tablespoons fresh chopped parsley

4. Add the garlic and cook for another minute. Deglaze with the Madeira wine and reduce almost completely. Add the veal stock and bring to a boil.

5. Return the chicken to the pan and any juices that accumulated in the bowl. Braise over very low heat for 2 hours, with the pan partly covered. (If the liquid is too thin, remove the lid to evaporate.)

6. Add the tomatoes, season with salt and pepper to taste, and sprinkle with the fresh parsley. Serve over white rice or *farofa* (page 128).

CHICKEN BEEF ROULADE

Enrolado de Bife com Frango

1 flank steak (about 1½ pounds)

2 teaspoons kosher salt, plus more for seasoning

freshly ground black pepper

¾ pound ground chicken

2 scallions (white and green parts), finely chopped

1 stalk celery, finely chopped

½ red onion, chopped

½ cup finely chopped yellow bell pepper

½ cup finely chopped red bell pepper

1 small carrot, finely diced

4 cloves garlic, minced

¼ cup fresh chopped parsley

3 tablespoons extra virgin olive oil

1 tablespoon soy sauce

1 chicken bouillon cube, grated into powder

Eronaria de Souza is from Goias, who grew up surrounded by yucca, pequi, guarana, turmeric, and all sorts of exotic foods. When I was hunting for recipes from this region, she told me about a meat stuffed with chicken, a specialty from Goias. At first, it seemed like an odd combination, but when I tasted it, I loved it. The roulade is slowly roasted and presents a spectrum of textures: crusty pulled meat around the edges and moist ground chicken stuffing packed with aromatic flavors in the center.

1. Trim the fat and silver skin from the steak. Butterfly the meat, working across the grain. Season with salt and pepper. Set aside.

2. Place the ground chicken in a large bowl. Stir in the scallions, celery, red onion, bell peppers, carrot, garlic, parsley, 1 tablespoon of the olive oil, the soy sauce, and bouillon cube. Season with salt and pepper. Spread inside the flank steak, making sure to leave a 2-inch edge on all sides. Roll up, making sure to fold some steak over the ends to avoid ground meat from escaping. Tie the roulade with string, making a knot in 5 to 6 places. Wrap in plastic wrap and refrigerate for 1 to 2 days.

3. Bring the roulade to room temperature at least 30 minutes before proceeding. Preheat the oven to 225°F.

4. Warm the remaining 2 tablespoons of olive oil in a large skillet over medium to high heat. Add the roulade and cook, rotating every 2 minutes, until it forms a brown crust all over, about 8 minutes total. Transfer to a cutting board and let rest for about 10 minutes.

5. Wrap the roulade in aluminum foil. Place seam side up on a baking sheet on the center rack of the oven. Cook for about 2 hours and save any juices that accumulate. Remove from the oven and let rest for 15 minutes.

6. Open the foil, pour any juices into a bowl, and place the meat onto a cutting board. Using a serrated knife, cut the meat into ¾-inch thick slices. Serve with the juices drizzled on top.

STEAK WITH FRIED EGGS

Bife à Cavalo

This simple meal is the combination of two strong proteins. It's the kind of meal that someone with a big appetite is looking for after a long day of work and exercise. Since I always have rice and beans on hand, I usually serve that as a side dish, or I serve this dish with a simple green salad and a small piece of bread, which is great for dipping in the oozing egg yolks and herbs. In Brazil, I usually make this dish using entrecôte or contrafilet, but this recipe can be easily applied to different cuts of meat. Rib-eye steaks work great. Bringing the meat to room temperature at least 30 minutes before cooking makes it a lot easier to cook.

four 8-ounce rib-eye steaks
kosher salt and freshly ground black pepper
2 tablespoons olive oil
4 tablespoons unsalted butter
4 eggs
1 shallot, finely chopped
2 tablespoons fresh chopped parsley
¼ cup Parmesan shavings

1   Season the steaks with salt and pepper on both sides. Pour the oil into a large sauté pan and sauté the meat over high heat until lightly brown and crispy on both sides, about 3 minutes per side. Remove the steaks from the pan and allow them to rest on a plate (depending on the thickness of the steak, you might need to place them in a preheated 350°F oven for 4 to 6 minutes).

2   Meanwhile, melt the butter in a medium non-stick skillet over medium heat. Crack each egg directly into the pan and season with salt and pepper. Cook until the egg whites are set but the yolks are still soft, 2 to 3 minutes.

3   As soon as the eggs are done, place each steak on a plate, and top with an egg.

4   Working fast over medium heat, add the shallot to the leftover butter in the pan. Swirl the pan around to make sure the shallot cooks lightly in the heat of the butter. Drizzle the shallot butter on top of each plate and garnish with the parsley and Parmesan shavings.

MEAT AND BLACK BEAN STEW

Feijoada

Feijoada is one of the most famous dishes in Brazil. Rio, my hometown, is the *feijoada* capital of Brazil, and every Saturday in Rio smells of it. This is a serious gastronomic dish, but a simple one: a big stew of black beans with lots of different kinds of succulent meats. It's served with white rice, *farofa* (page 128), collard greens, and orange slices. *Feijoada*, like any stew, takes a few hours to prepare; however, it can handle a bit of neglect and still deliver an impressive result—just keep the temperature low at all times. As the beans simmer, the stew will get thicker and a glossy film should form on the top. Adjusting the consistency of the *feijoada* is easy: If it's too thick, add a bit of water and if it's too thin, simmer with the pan uncovered. Feel free to season with Tabasco, Worcestershire sauce, nutmeg, or paprika.

1   Place the beans in a very large pot and cover with cold water. Bring to a boil over high heat. Turn the heat down to medium, and cook, covered, for 1 hour, until the beans are just cooked but not too mushy. Set aside. (You can cook the beans in a pressure cooker if you want to save time, and it will only take you 15 to 25 minutes.)

2   Meanwhile, start preparing the meats and vegetables. Sauté the oxtail, top round, and sausage, in batches, until browned on all sides. Transfer to a large bowl and cover tightly with aluminum foil.

3   Heat the oil in a large Dutch oven pan and cook the pancetta until lightly crispy. Add the onion, celery, leeks, shallots, and scallions and cook, stirring occasionally, until tender, 3 to 5 minutes. Add the garlic and stir to blend with the other vegetables. Add the beans and bay leaves and bring to a boil. Add the meats and any accumulated juices from the bowl. Season very lightly with salt and pepper and cover the pan. Simmer at low heat for about 3 hours, until the meats are tender and falling off the bones. Taste and adjust the seasoning again.

4   Serve with rice, *farofa*, collard greens, and a simple orange grapefruit salad.

MAKES 8 TO 10 SERVINGS

4 cups dried black beans, picked and rinsed

4 pieces oxtail, about 1¼ pounds

1 pound top round, cut into big chunks

1 chorizo sausage, about 1 pound

1 tablespoon canola oil

½ pound pancetta, cut into 1-inch cubes

½ cup chopped onion

½ cup chopped celery

½ cup chopped leeks

½ cup chopped shallot

½ cup chopped scallions

2 tablespoons minced garlic

3 bay leaves

kosher salt and freshly ground black pepper

CHOOSING MEAT

Pig's feet? Pig's ears? Beef cheeks? In a traditional *feijoada,* any piece of meat from any kind of animal (pork parts, beef parts, *carne seca*, and linguiça are the most common) can release a bit of flavor is thrown in the pan, even if it's just for the sake of flavor as I do when I use pig's ears. (I remove the ears just before serving.) There is a world of meats beyond steaks, ribs, and shoulders to explore and this is the perfect dish to venture into the land of unfamiliar cuts. Your best bet for finding these are a good butcher or ethnic markets, including Brazilian, of course. If the dish is too salty, transfer the meats from the beans. In my own interpretation of *feijoada*, the meats are sautéed before adding them to the beans. I think searing meats add a great flavor.

VEAL FILET MIGNON

Filet Mignon de Vitela com

In the pastry world, there are lots of caramel sauces based on caramelized sugar that is "uncooked" with heavy cream, fruit juice, or other liquid. In designing this unexpected recipe for catering a Brazilian party, I thought to myself: What would happen if I caramelized sugar and uncooked it with veal stock? The sauce that resulted is the most velvety veal stock I've ever tasted. It has a light touch of sweetness, a great consistency, and the most beautiful brown color. Beef stock is an acceptable substitute but not nearly as perfect. The filet mignon of veal is something you may have to special-order from your butcher, or you can purchase it at www.creativemeats.com. Pork tenderloin is a good substitute. Although endives are often found in salad mixes or raw hors d'oeuvres, they take a completely different turn when cooked. The texture changes from crisp to creamy, and the bitterness changes to mild and sweet. Fennel is a solid alternative.

MAKES 4 SERVINGS

2 cups veal stock
¼ cup, plus 2 tablespoons sugar
2 tablespoons water
¼ cup heavy cream
kosher salt and freshly ground black pepper
⅛ teaspoon fresh lemon juice

4 endives, about 1 pound
1 tablespoon unsalted butter

2 veal or pork filet mignons
   (total weight 1½ pounds)
2 tablespoons canola oil

---

1 Bring the veal stock to a simmer in a medium saucepan.

2 Place ¼ cup plus 1 tablespoon of the sugar and water in a large saucepan and cook over high heat, until the sugar turns a dark amber caramel color, 2 to 3 minutes. Add the veal stock all at once. Reduce the heat to low, and simmer until it reduces by half and thickens, about 15 minutes.

3 Add the heavy cream, whisk lightly, and cook the sauce until the cream is well blended, about 2 minutes. Season with salt and pepper, and lemon juice. This can be prepared up to 3 days ahead of time and kept in the refrigerator in an airtight plastic container.

4 Prepare the endives by removing any limp outer leaves, then slice in half lengthwise. Place in a large skillet with the butter. Add ¾

cup of water and season with salt and pepper. Cook, partly covered, over low heat until tender, about 5 minutes. Uncover the pan to allow any remaining water to evaporate, but make sure the endives don't dry out.

5 Using a pair of tongs, carefully lift the endives so you can add 1 tablespoon of sugar to the bottom of the pan. Cook until the sugar starts to caramelize. Add another ¼ cup of water and turn the heat to high, swirling the pan around and making sure the endives are lightly coated. Cook until the liquid evaporates. Season with salt and pepper and keep warm.

6 Preheat the oven to 375°F. Trim any silver skin from the veal and season with salt and pepper.

7 Heat the oil in an ovenproof skillet over medium heat, and swirl to coat the bottom. Add the veal and cook, until golden brown, about 6 minutes. Place the skillet in the oven to finish cooking the meat until it's medium done, 5 to 6 minutes. Remove from the oven and let rest for 5 minutes before slicing.

8. Cut the meat on a bias across the grain into ½-inch-thick slices. Place an endive and a few slices of filet mignon on a warm plate, and top everything with the caramel sauce.

GRILLED CACHAÇA MARINATED HANGER STEAK

Fraldinha Marinada na Cachaça e Grelhada

This is a great recipe for grilling. The marinade has a real wow factor, as the cachaça adds a unique spicy flavor to the steak. If you cannot find cachaça, vodka also works. Marinades are one of my favorite ways to tenderize meats and they add tons of flavor. Keep in mind that with all marinades, time is your best ally. If you can marinate the meat for two to three days, then do so—it will only make the taste even better. I have also prepared lamb using this marinade and it turned out wonderfully.

MAKES 2 TO 4 SERVINGS

1 medium onion, thinly sliced
3 cloves garlic, roughly chopped
1 teaspoon ketchup
1 teaspoon coriander seeds
1 tablespoon honey
1 teaspoon soy sauce
¼ cup cachaça
½ cup canola or olive oil
1 hanger steak, about 1 pound
kosher salt and freshly ground black pepper

1   In a large bowl, whisk all the ingredients for the marinade. Place the meat in a large ziplock bag and pour the marinade into the bag. Rub the marinade around the meat until it is well distributed. Remove all the air from the plastic bag and seal it well. Place the meat in the refrigerator in such a position so that it is covered by the marinade and let it rest for at least 12 hours, preferably 2 to 3 days.

2   Preheat the grill on high heat for at least 10 minutes before cooking. Remove the meat from the marinade and wipe off the remaining specks of onion, garlic, and coriander.

3   Season the meat with salt and pepper on both sides and place it on the hot grill. If you want to create an attractive crosshatch grill mark, grill for 2 minutes and rotate the meat 45 degrees from its original position, then grill for another 2 minutes; do this on each side. Depending on the thickness of the meat, leave it cooking on the grill for 4 to 5 minutes on each side, turning sides once. If you like your meat rare or well done, adjust the cooking time according to your taste (see below). A meat thermometer is always a good tool when seeking precisely the right doneness.

HANGER STEAK TEMPERATURE GUIDELINES

Blue – 120°F
Rare – 125°F
Medium rare – 135°F
Medium – 145°F
Medium well – 155°F
Well done – 170°F

BRAZILIAN BEEF RAGÙ

Picadinho

2 tablespoons vegetable or canola oil
2 pounds beef shoulder, cut into ¼-inch pieces
kosher salt and freshly ground black pepper
2 tablespoons olive oil
1½ ounces pancetta, cut into ¼-inch pieces
½ cup finely chopped onion
3 scallions (white and green parts), finely chopped
½ cup finely chopped red bell pepper
½ cup finely chopped yellow bell pepper
½ cup finely chopped green bell pepper
5 cloves garlic, finely minced
¾ cup red wine (such as Cabernet Sauvignon
    or Zinfandel)
2 tablespoons tomato paste
2 cups veal stock
2 teaspoons Worcestershire sauce
pinch of ground nutmeg
pinch of cayenne pepper
2 plum tomatoes, peeled, seeded, and diced
3 tablespoons fresh chopped parsley

Picadinho is a staple of Brazilian cooking much like Bolognese is in Italian cuisine. Cut the bell peppers very small since you want them to almost disappear while cooking, but their sweetness will be impossible to ignore. Feel free to use different kinds of meat such as lamb and veal. In Brazil, they don't use bacon or pancetta to make *picadinho*, but I think it adds immense flavor to the dish. You can serve *picadinho* with pasta or with rice or mashed potatoes. If you want to really hold to Brazilian tradition you can serve it with *farofa* (page 128).

1   Heat the oil in a large heavy-bottomed saucepan over high heat. Season the beef with salt and pepper and add to the pan in batches, if necessary, so you don't overcrowd, and cook until cooked through, about 3 to 5 minutes. Transfer to a bowl and cover with aluminum foil so no steam escapes.

2   Place the olive oil and pancetta in the same pan. Cook over medium heat, stirring, until lightly crispy, 2 to 3 minutes.

3   Reduce the heat to low and add the onion, scallions, and peppers. Cook, stirring frequently, until the vegetables become soft and tender, about 3 minutes. Add the garlic and cook while stirring, for another minute.

4   Transfer the beef and all accumulated juices to the pan and stir. Pour in the wine and simmer until it has reduced by a little more then half, about 5 minutes. Add the tomato paste, veal stock, and Worcestershire sauce. Season lightly with salt, pepper, nutmeg, and cayenne. Cover and simmer over very low heat for 1 to 1½ hours.

5   Adjust the seasoning, add the tomatoes, and simmer for 3 minutes. Spoon the *picadinho* over your starch of choice and garnish with the fresh parsley.

GROUND MEAT AND CREAMY CORN PIE

Torta de Carne e Pamonha

Strongly rooted in indigenous cooking and similar to tamales in Mexico, *pamonha* is a paste made from puréed corn and milk, which is wrapped and steamed inside corn-husks. In Brazil, this street food is prepared either sweet with sugar and cinnamon or savory with cheese. I was inspired to create a Brazilian version of shepherd's pie when I recently ate a savory *pamonha* in Brazil and realized that a creamy and cheesy corn crust would be the perfect topping for a layer of ground meat. I first developed this recipe in Brazil, using fresh corn, dry polenta, milk, and Parmesan for the topping. I was later inspired by the Mexican combination of cheddar over ground meats and chiles, and the pie tastes even better this way. This can be prepared well ahead of serving.

2 tablespoons olive oil

¼ pound pancetta, finely diced

½ cup chopped onion

½ cup chopped scallions

½ cup chopped carrots

½ cup chopped celery

2 cloves garlic, chopped

1¼ pounds ground beef

⅓ cup white wine

½ cup tomato paste

1 cup whole milk

1 cup water

kosher salt and freshly ground black pepper

2 tablespoons fresh chopped parsley

1 cup corn kernels, fresh, canned, or frozen and thawed

2 tablespoons unsalted butter

1 cup yellow cornmeal (dry polenta)

1 tablespoon baking powder

1 cup sour cream

1½ cups yellow sharp cheddar

7 x 11 baking dish

1. Heat the olive oil in a large, heavy-bottomed saucepan over medium to high heat and add the pancetta. Cook, stirring, until lightly crispy, about 3 minutes. Add the onion, scallions, carrots, and celery and cook, stirring frequently, until soft and tender, about 3 minutes. Add the garlic and cook for another minute. Add the ground beef to the pan and break the meat into tiny bits until completely cooked through, 6 to 8 minutes.

2. Add the wine and reduce by half, about 3 minutes. Add the tomato paste, milk, and water. Stir gently and cook, partly covered, for 1 hour over low heat.

3. Season with salt and pepper and sprinkle with the fresh parsley. Transfer to the baking dish, spread with a spatula, and cool at room temperature.

4. Meanwhile, place the corn in the bowl of a food processor and purée into a smooth paste.

5. Melt the butter in a medium saucepan over low heat. Add the cornmeal and mix until the polenta becomes slightly wet. Add the puréed corn and stir over low heat until it looks like a coarse meal, about 1 minute. Immediately transfer to a large bowl.

6. Add the baking powder and mix well. Add the sour cream and 1 cup of the cheese, and mash everything together until it forms a dough. Season with salt and pepper.

7. Preheat the oven to 375°F. On a lightly floured surface, use a rolling pin or your hands to make the dough into a rectangle, about the size of the baking dish. Carefully lift the dough with your hands and place it on top of the baking dish, making sure the meat layer is all covered.

8. Sprinkle the remaining ½ cup of cheddar cheese on top. Bake the pie in the oven until the cheese is bubbling and the top is golden brown, 20 to 25 minutes.

9. Remove from the oven and let it rest at room temperature for 10 minutes before serving.

LAMB STEW WITH YUCCA AND TURMERIC

Cozido de Carneiro, Aipim e Açafrão-da-Terra

Although Brazil is generally hot, when it comes to comfort foods, we inherited a taste for stews. This recipe is inspired by the flavors of Goiás, located in the center of Brazil, where they use lots of lamb, yucca, and turmeric. The yucca infuses the stock with a uniquely earthy element. I recommend using veal stock, but if you have access to homemade or fresh-from-the-butcher lamb stock, go for that. Lamb shoulder is my favorite cut of meat because it is tender and full of flavor, but a leg of lamb is fine, too.

MAKES 6 TO 8 SERVINGS

3 pounds lamb shoulder, fat trimmed, cut into
   1½- to 2-inch pieces
kosher salt and freshly ground black pepper
2 yucca (about ½ pound each)
4 tablespoons olive oil
½ cup white wine
2 medium onions, finely chopped
3 small carrots, cut into large chunks
2 stalks celery, cut into large chunks
10 cloves garlic, finely minced
2 teaspoons turmeric
4 cups veal (or lamb) stock
¼ cup fresh chopped cilantro

1   Place the meat on a tray and season with salt and pepper. Cover loosely with plastic wrap and let come to room temperature.

2   Prepare the yucca as on page 32.

3   Pour 2 tablespoons of the olive oil into a large heavy-bottomed pan and swirl to coat the entire bottom. Add the lamb and cook in batches, over medium heat, until browned, 3 to 5 minutes. Transfer to a bowl and cover with aluminum foil.

4   Add the wine to the pan and bring to a full boil, then pour it over the meat and cover the bowl again.

5   Wipe the pan and add the remaining 2 tablespoons of olive oil. Stir in the chopped onions, carrots, and celery. Cook until soft, about 3 minutes. Stir in the garlic and cook another minute. Stir in the turmeric. Add the lamb with all the juices that accumulated in the bowl. Add enough veal stock to cover the pieces of meat and vegetables, and bring to a boil, then reduce the heat to low.

6   Drain the yucca pieces from the water and add them to the pot. Braise at a gentle simmer, either on top of the stove or in a 300°F oven, until the meat is very tender and the yucca is cooked but not mushy, 2½ to 3 hours. Turn off the heat and let the stew settle for a few minutes.

7   Discard the chunks of carrots and celery. Season with salt and pepper. Garnish with the fresh cilantro.

DUCK RICE
Arroz de Pato

I eat duck rice quite often in Brazil. It's a classic Portuguese dish sometimes prepared in the style of fried rice, other times prepared in the style of risotto. I could never really pick which was my favorite way—until I dined at Aldea, Portuguese chef Georges Mendez's new restaurant. When the duck rice arrived, I felt like culture was singing to me. In his version, chef Mendez prepares the dish using a paella technique. Mixed in with the rice are pulled meat from a duck confit, thinly sliced chorizo, and black olives. This version is inspired by chef Mendez's, but I took a real shortcut here by using ready-made duck confit. It's a step that takes you there just a little faster than if you were making your own.

2 duck legs confit, ready-made
3 tablespoons extra virgin olive oil
1 small, thin chorizo sausage (about ¼ pound), cut on a bias into thin slices
3 cups chicken stock
⅓ cup finely chopped onion
3 cloves garlic, finely minced
pinch of saffron threads
½ teaspoon paprika
1 plum tomato, peeled, seeded, and diced
1 cup Spanish rice
kosher salt and freshly ground black pepper
⅛ cup Kalamata olives, pitted and sliced

1   Preheat the oven to 375°F.

2   Warm the duck legs and fat gently in a skillet over low heat. Separate the legs from the fat and let cool to room temperature. Use your fingers to shred the meat and save the fat for other uses. Set aside.

3   Heat 1 tablespoon of olive oil in a small sauté pan and add the choriço, cooking until lightly browned, about 2 minutes. Transfer to a plate, cover with aluminum foil, and set aside.

4   Bring the chicken stock to a simmer in a saucepan.

5   Heat the remaining olive oil in a large skillet over medium heat. Add the onion and garlic, and cook until slightly golden. Add the saffron and paprika and cook for another minute. Stir in the diced tomato and cook until soft, about 2 minutes. Add the rice and stir well to coat, making sure it's spread evenly around the pan. Add the stock and bring to a boil. Season lightly with salt and pepper.

6   Add the duck meat and chorizo, and stir just once (if you stir later in the process, the rice gets sticky). Place the skillet in the oven and cook until the rice is cooked but not mushy, 8 to 10 minutes.

7   Remove the skillet from the oven. Taste and adjust the seasoning, mix in the olives, and serve hot.

CHICKEN STOCK Caldo de Galinha

1 to 2 pounds of chicken bones (from any
    part of the chicken)
1 onion, peeled and quartered
1 carrot, peeled and cut into chunks
1 stalk celery, cut into chunks
2 cloves garlic, peeled
1 teaspoon black peppercorns, cracked
A few sprigs of thyme
A few sprigs of parsley
2 to 3 bay leaves

1   Remove the excess fat from the bones (especially if you are starting with raw bones). Place them in a large stockpot and cover with cold water, 3 to 4 cups, or 1 to 2 inches above the bones. Don't try to add too much water, or the stock will be too watery and lack flavor. Bring to a boil over high heat. At this point change the water if it's bloody, or continue on by reducing the heat to low and simmer at a very gentle heat for about 30 minutes, skimming the foam occasionally.

2   Add the vegetables and herbs, and simmer for another 15 minutes, skimming occasionally.

3   Taste the stock. When it has a rich chicken flavor, remove the bones, vegetables, and herbs with a slotted spoon and strain the stock, first through a medium strainer, then through a fine mesh sieve.

4   Place the stock over an ice bath, then chill in the refrigerator for 12 to 24 hours – chilled is the best way to judge the quality of the stock. The more gelatinous, the better. Carefully remove any fat that accumulates on the top and discard it. Divide the stock into several small plastic containers, label them, and store in the refrigerator for up to 4 days or in the freezer for up to 4 months.

SHRIMP STOCK Caldo de Camarao

2 tablespoons olive oil
Shells from 2 pounds shrimp
1 large onion, peeled and quartered
1 stalk celery, cut into chunks
1 small carrot, peeled and cut into chunks
3 cloves garlic, peeled
2 bay leaves
A few sprigs of thyme
A few sprigs of parsley

1   Heat the oil in a large heavy-bottomed saucepan over medium heat. Add the shells and cook until they turn bright orange, 3 to 5 minutes. Add the vegetables and cook until they start to soften, 2 to 3 minutes.

2   Pour 4 to 6 cups of water just slightly above the shells, and reduce the heat to low. Add the herbs and simmer at a very low heat for about 30 minutes, skimming the foam occasionally.

3   Remove the shells, vegetables, and herbs with a slotted spoon and strain through a fine-mesh sieve. Place the stock over an ice bath, then chill in the refrigerator. Divide the stock into airtight plastic containers, label them, and store in the refrigerator for up to 2 days or in the freezer for up to 3 months.

VEAL STOCK Caldo de Vitela

6 pounds veal bones
3 carrots, peeled and cut into chunks
2 onions, peeled and quartered
5 cloves garlic, peeled
¼ cup tomato paste
1 tablespoon black peppercorns, cracked
A few sprigs of thyme
A few sprigs of parsley
3 to 4 bay leaves

1   Preheat the oven to 450°F. Place the veal bones in a large roasting pan, but do not overcrowd them. Roast until medium brown on one side, about 30 minutes, then turn them upside down (remove any accumulated fat at this point) and continue to roast for another 30 minutes.

2   Transfer the bones to a large stockpot and cover them with 4 to 6 quarts of cold water just 1 to 2 inches above the bones. Cover and cook over high heat just to bring to a boil, about 15 minutes. Uncover, reduce the heat to low, and cook at a very gentle simmer, skimming occasionally. Do not try to rush the process by raising the heat and boiling. You want very small bubbles at the most.

3   When the bones have cooked for about 4 hours, add the vegetables, tomato paste, peppercorns, and herbs. Continue to simmer for another 2 hours, skimming occasionally.

4   Remove the big bones, vegetables, and herbs from the stockpot with a slotted spoon and strain the stock, first through a medium strainer, then through a fine mesh sieve. Place the stock over an ice bath, then chill in the refrigerator for 12 to 24 hours. Carefully discard any fat that accumulates on the top. Divide the stock into several small plastic containers, label them, and store in the refrigerator for up to 4 days or in the freezer for up to 6 months.

Side Dishes
Acompanhamentos

RICE AND BEANS

Arroz e Feião

Brazil is a rice-and-bean nation. This duo is the backbone of every household in the country. When it comes to the basics, Brazilians count on ordinary white rice. In the United States, I like basmati and jasmine, and you can use either one for this recipe. Brazilians like their rice quite loose, never sticky, and that's why we wash it beforehand. We also never stir during the cooking process. As for the beans, black beans rule in Brazil, but feel free to use other types of beans such as red kidney or pinto. When looking for a meaty or smoky flavor in your beans, you can add bacon or sausage. The flavor of cooked beans does improve after a day or two in the refrigerator. The beans cook in two easy steps. First, in the pressure cooker. Second, in a regular saucepan with onions, garlic, and seasonings. One pot of cooked beans can last for 3 to 4 days and it's definitely something you can make ahead of time. Beans tend to get creamier when resting in the refrigerator, so, by all means, adjust the consistency by adding a little bit of water or stock.

MAKES 6 TO 8 SERVINGS

2 cups white rice (such as basmati or jasmine)
2 teaspoons kosher salt
4 tablespoons extra virgin olive oil
2 cloves garlic, minced, plus 1 tablespoon, finely minced
1 pound dried black beans, picked over and rinsed (but not soaked)
1 medium onion, finely chopped
kosher salt and freshly ground black pepper
3 fresh bay leaves
1 to 2 teaspoons Worcestershire sauce

1 Rinse the rice in cold water to wash away the excess starch.

2 Bring 3 cups of water, the rice, salt, 2 tablespoons of the olive oil, and 2 cloves minced garlic to a boil in a heavy saucepan, tightly covered. Reduce the heat to a gentle simmer and cook, covered, until the rice is tender and the water is absorbed, 15 to 20 minutes.

3 Remove from the heat and let stand, uncovered, for 5 minutes. Fluff with a fork.

4 Place the black beans in a pressure cooker and cover with tap water by 2 inches. Lock the lid and bring to a boil. When you hear the sound of the pressure cooker in full gear, reduce the heat to medium-low. (It is very important to maintain a constant gentle pressure because the pressure keeps increasing as the boiling point of the water increases.) Check the beans after 25 to 30 minutes; they

should be tender, but not mushy. The water will be dark but still clear. Remove from the heat and set aside.

5   Pour the remaining 2 tablespoons of olive oil into a saucepan and cook the onion over medium heat until soft, about 3 minutes. Add 1 tablespoon of finely minced garlic and cook until golden brown, about 2 minutes. Immediately pour the beans and liquid into the pan, then add the salt and pepper and bay leaves. Simmer the beans on a gentle heat until the liquid becomes thicker and glossy, 15 to 20 minutes. Check the seasoning and add the Worcestershire sauce to taste. Serve over the rice.

PRESSURE COOKERS

Pressure cookers have a relevant cultural value in Brazil, since they symbolize the importance of beans. They are used every day and make life a lot easier, reducing cooking time from 2 hours in a regular pan to just 30 to 40 minutes. The idea behind a pressure cooker is that no air or liquid can escape, creating pressure and making cooking a lot faster. Never open a pressure cooker without releasing the pressure first. To do this, lift up the center handle until all the steam—or pressure—is released. You can also place the pot under running water. Read the instructions of your pressure cooker before using since each brand may differ slightly.

THREE BEAN RISOTTO

Risotto de Três Feijões

This intriguing risotto is a creative way to serve one of the most internationally loved comfort foods with Brazilian flair. You want the proper risotto texture: creamy rice that is wet, loose, and runny, not thick and pasty. Then add the flavors of Brazil with *carne seca* and beans. Although I am using three different kinds of beans, feel free to use more or fewer varieties, and I use canned to save time. If you are left with extra beans, use them in soups, salads, casseroles, or stews. As for the jerk meat, you can use bacon or pancetta as substitutes. Note that the jerk meat is not being desalted so it will infuse the risotto with plenty of saltiness. Try to use a low-sodium chicken stock and taste the risotto before adding any additional seasoning. This flexible dish can be served as an appetizer, a main course, or a side dish.

1   In a medium saucepan, bring the chicken stock to a simmer.

2   Heat the olive oil in a large, heavy saucepan over medium heat and add the jerk meat. Cook, stirring occasionally, until the meat browns and turns lightly crispy, about 3 minutes. Add the onion and cook, stirring frequently, until soft and translucent, about 2 minutes. Add the rice and stir frequently until the grains are warm and coated with the onion and meat mixture, about 3 minutes. Add the wine and simmer, stirring constantly, until the liquid is absorbed, about 1 minute.

MAKES 4 SERVINGS

3½ cups chicken stock

1 tablespoon extra virgin olive oil, plus extra for garnish

2 ounces jerk meat, finely diced (about ½ cup)

½ medium onion, finely diced

1 cup Arborio rice

⅛ cup dry white wine

⅛ cup canned black beans, drained and rinsed

⅛ cup canned red kidney beans, drained and rinsed

⅛ cup canned roman beans, drained and rinsed

2 tablespoons unsalted butter

kosher salt and freshly ground black pepper

2 tablespoons fresh chopped tarragon

3   Slowly add one ladle of simmering stock and allow the rice to cook, stirring often, until the liquid is absorbed. Adjust the heat to maintain a gentle simmer. Add another ladle, and repeat the process. Continue adding ladles of stock only when the previous addition has been completely absorbed. Cook until the rice is tender but still firm to the bite, 18 to 20 minutes. Season lightly with salt if necessary.

4   Add the beans and butter and fold into the rice. Don't let the risotto get too thick; if the rice seems to have absorbed all of the liquid, add another tablespoon of chicken stock to achieve the right creamy consistency. Taste and adjust the seasoning if necessary.

5   Sprinkle the tarragon over the risotto and spoon it onto warm plates. Serve immediately while the risotto is still hot.

EGG STUFFED BAKED POTATO

Batatas Recheadas com Ovo

The potatoes in this recipe are served whole: stuffed with mashed potatoes, topped with an egg, drenched in heavy cream, and dusted with Parmesan cheese. So many textures and tastes—crunchy, smooth, rich, buttery, salty, custardy, cheesy—all in one dish. Not to mention you get those extra vitamins from the skin. I like to serve these potatoes with the yolks very runny, but feel free to cook for a few more minutes for a firmer yolk. This is the perfect side dish for a chicken or beef dish, or it can serve as the main course with a green salad. Make sure to buy potatoes of the same size and with a nice oval shape.

1   Preheat the oven to 350°F.

2   Wash the potatoes in cold water and rub the skin to remove any dirt. Dry each potato with a paper towel. Place them in the oven and bake the potatoes until tender and a knife inserted in the middle goes in easily, 30 to 40 minutes.

3   Remove from the oven, and while they are still hot, cut a top horizontally, following the oval shape. Using a towel to hold the hot potato, scoop out most of the potato flesh with a spoon, leaving the sides and the bottom with a thin layer of potato to hold its shape. Place the scooped potato through a ricer or food mill.

MAKES 4 SERVINGS

4 medium Yukon potatoes,
5 tablespoons unsalted butter, at room temperature
⅓ cup whole milk, hot
kosher salt and freshly ground black pepper
pinch of ground nutmeg
4 large eggs
4 teaspoons heavy cream
4 tablespoons freshly grated Parmesan

4   Add the butter and mix. Add the hot milk, a little at a time, and mix until well blended. Season with salt, pepper, and fresh nutmeg.

5   Transfer the mashed potatoes to a pastry bag or ziplock bag and cut the tip. Fill the baked potatoes halfway with the mashed potato mixture, leaving space for the egg. You might have some extra mashed potatoes left in the pastry bag.

6   One at a time, break the eggs and carefully remove about 1 tablespoon of the egg whites with a spoon and discard. Pour each remaining egg intact inside each potato. Season with salt and pepper.

7   Add 1 teaspoon of heavy cream to each potato and sprinkle 1 tablespoon of Parmesan on top. Bake the potatoes until the whites are just set but the yolks are still runny, 6 to 8 minutes.

ROASTED POTATOES WITH BAY LEAVES

Batatinhas Assadas com Louro

While the French use a lot of duck fat to make confits, Brazilians make good use of chicken fat. Fast and easy to prepare, it pairs perfectly with young potatoes. I never pass up the opportunity to make rendered fat from chicken skin (see below). I end up with a batch of cracklings that are irresistible to snack on. If you don't want to make chicken fat, feel free to use duck fat, which is a lot easier to find. The combination of potatoes and bay leaves is classic in Brazil and Portugal, but you could also use rosemary or thyme. I love to serve it with grilled meat, such as the hanger steak marinated in cachaça on page 106).

MAKES 4 SERVINGS

12 small yellow potatoes, about 1½ pounds total
¼ cup chicken fat, melted and cooled
6 large cloves garlic, peeled and whole
10 bay leaves (preferably fresh)
kosher salt and freshly ground black pepper

CHICKEN (OR DUCK) FAT

Trim off the skin and fat from 1 whole chicken (or duck). Cut into medium pieces and put into a heavy-bottomed saucepan. Cook, uncovered, over low heat. As the fat begins to melt, strain it through a colander into a bowl and return the skin pieces to continue cooking at low heat until they are crisp and have released all of their fat. Strain the clear liquid through a sieve and let cool. You will have ½ to ¾ cups from a chicken, 1 to 1⅓ cups from a duck. Store in an airtight plastic container for up to 6 weeks in the refrigerator or 3 months in the freezer.

1   Preheat the oven to 375°F.

2   Wash the potatoes in cold water and scrub the skin to remove any dirt. Dry with paper towels and cut the potatoes into large chunks.

3   Place the potatoes in a large bowl and pour the chicken fat over. Stir carefully with a rubber spatula, making sure each potato chunk is well coated with fat.

4   Add the garlic cloves and bay leaves. Season with salt and pepper and stir again.

5   Place the potatoes in a large roasting pan and place them in the oven. Bake until they are tender and golden brown, 30 to 35 minutes, stirring the potatoes every 10 minutes.

COLLARD GREENS
Couve Mineira Refogada

Collard greens may be Brazil's most popular green vegetable, and an obligatory side dish served with *feijoada*. Vegetables in Brazil are seldom just steamed and collard greens are no exception. Onions and/or garlic are always present as the basic accompaniments, but collards work well with a range of seasonings and make an excellent addition to pasta sauces, soups, and egg dishes. When shopping for collards, choose dark green ones with firm stems and no discolorations. Unlike other vegetables that turn into mush when overcooked, collard greens are very forgiving—it's quite hard to overcook them. If you like crispy collards, toss the leaves in some oil with onions. When you add liquid, you lose brightness but gain tenderness. In this recipe, I suggest braising with a small quantity of water, but feel free to add any kind of stock instead, and even a piece of smoked meat to oomph the flavor.

MAKES 4 SERVINGS

1 bunch of collard greens (1½ to 2 pounds)
2 tablespoons extra virgin olive oil
½ onion, minced
kosher salt and freshly ground black pepper

1 Trim the stems and the thick center ribs from the collard green leaves. Choose some of the thickest stems; peel them to remove the thick fiber and chop them roughly. Set aside.

2 Stack a few leaves and roll them tightly into a cigar shape. Cut them into very thin strips crosswise and place in a bowl. Repeat with the remaining leaves.

3 Pour the olive oil into a large pan. Add the onion and cook over medium heat, stirring occasionally, until soft and translucent, about 2 minutes. Add the collard greens and toss them, making sure all the leaves are well coated with the oil and onion mixture. Season with salt and pepper. Add 1 cup of water, cover the pan, and reduce the heat to low. Simmer gently until the leaves are soft, about 10 minutes. Drain any excess liquid before serving.

CARROTS WITH PINEAPPLE SAUCE AND GOLDEN RAISINS

Cenoura com Molho de Abacaxi e Passas

This recipe is inspired by the wonderful salads I used to eat at Celeiro, a restaurant famous in Rio for just that. When marinated in a pineapple and raisin sauce, shredded carrots become crunchy and tender, receiving both sweet and sour notes. The three ingredients harmonize nicely and the result is very refreshing and healthy. Try to use a fresh and fragrant pineapple and organic and crispy carrots for this recipe. Feel free to use dark raisins instead of golden if that's what you prefer. Bring this to a barbecue instead of potato salad or coleslaw, and be prepared for compliments!

MAKES 4 SERVINGS

2 cups finely diced fresh pineapple

⅓ cup water

⅓ cup golden raisins

2 teaspoons Dijon mustard

1 teaspoon white wine vinegar

kosher salt and freshly ground black pepper

pinch of turmeric

pinch of cinnamon

¾ pound carrots (4 to 5 carrots), peeled and trimmed

2 tablespoons mayonnaise

¼ cup fresh chopped chives

1   Place 1 cup of pineapple with ⅓ cup of water in a blender, and blend until the fruit is completely liquefied, about 2 minutes. Strain the juice through a fine sieve into a measuring cup and keep 1 cup. If need be, press the pulp to extract more juice, then discard the pulp.

2   Bring the pineapple juice to a simmer in a medium saucepan, over low heat. Add the remaining 1 cup of diced pineapple, raisins, mustard, and vinegar. Cook over very low heat, stirring occasionally, until the raisins soften and the mustard dissolves in the juice, 3 to 5 minutes. Season with salt and pepper, turmeric, and cinnamon. Transfer to a bowl and let cool.

3   Meanwhile, grate the carrots using the largest holes in your grater. Place the grated carrots in a bowl.

4   When the pineapple sauce is cooled, fold in the mayonnaise with a rubber spatula. Pour the pineapple sauce over the carrots and fold everything together.

5   Chill the salad in the refrigerator for at least 1 hour. Remove it from the refrigerator at least 20 minutes before serving. Garnish with the fresh chopped chives.

ASPARAGUS WITH SHALLOT AND PARSLEY SAUCE

Asparagus com Molho de Echallote e Salsinha

This dish is a light and elegant side dish for meat or fish. In Brazil, fresh asparagus is considered a fancy vegetable and the herb-shallot sauce only elevates its bright, fresh flavor. When I can, I like to mix white and green asparagus, but when I don't have the white on hand, I use fresh hearts of palm. Both taste wonderful with this sauce.

MAKES 4 SERVINGS

1 pound asparagus
3 tablespoons salt
¼ teaspoon baking soda
1 tablespoon olive oil
1 slice of bacon, finely chopped
2 small shallots, finely chopped
1 cup chicken stock
2 tablespoons unsalted butter, cold, cut into pieces
kosher salt and freshly ground black pepper
2 tablespoons fresh chopped parsley
¼ cup freshly grated Parmesan

1 Cut the woody bottoms off the asparagus and peel it, leaving the flower part intact.

2 Bring a large pot of water to a boil. Add the salt and baking soda. Submerge the asparagus in the water and cook until they just become soft. Immediately transfer them to an ice bath and then let them cool completely. Remove from the ice bath and let them dry on paper towels.

3 In a medium sauté pan, add the olive oil and bacon and cook over medium heat until lightly crispy, about 2 minutes. Lower the heat and add the shallots, stirring occasionally, being careful not to brown them, about 2 minutes. Add the chicken stock and reduce by half, about 5 minutes.

4 Lift the saucepan a few inches above the heat and add the cold pieces of butter. Shake the pan back and forth until the butter is melted and incorporated into the sauce. Season with salt and pepper. Add the asparagus to the pan and reheat over very low heat, being careful not to boil the sauce. Add the parsley.

5 Transfer the asparagus and sauce to a plate and serve with the Parmesan sprinkled on top.

BROCCOLI AND MINAS CHEESE SOUFFLÉ

Soufflé de Broccolis e Queijo Minas

This is a different kind of soufflé, one that can withstand a 24-hour resting period easily because the egg whites are not whipped. Whole eggs are added to a healthy and refreshing broccoli and Minas base. You can also substitute brocollini or broccoli rabe. They all come from the same family but have different degrees of bitterness, from the mildest broccoli to the most bitter broccoli rabe (which is great to pair with sausages). In Brazil we often serve soufflés as a side dish for protein, but feel free to serve it as a lunch or a light dinner with a green salad. I like to bake these in individual ramekins, four ounces in size.

MAKES 6 TO 8 SERVINGS

2 cups whole milk

6 tablespoons butter, more for ramekins

6 tablespoons all-purpose flour

kosher salt and freshly ground black pepper

pinch of ground nutmeg

pinch of cayenne pepper

5 whole eggs

2 cups grated Minas cheese (about ½ pound)

1⅓ cups chopped cooked broccoli

¼ cup grated Parmesan

---

1   Preheat the oven to 375°F. Lightly coat the insides of the ramekins with melted butter.

2   Bring the milk to a light simmer in a small saucepan.

3   Melt the butter in a medium saucepan over low heat. Add the flour, whisk well, and cook until it's blended, about 1 minute. Add the warm milk all at once and whisk well until it's a smooth béchamel sauce. Season with salt and pepper, nutmeg, and cayenne. Transfer to a bowl and let cool at room temperature for 10 to 15 minutes.

4   Break all the eggs in a small bowl, season with a small pinch of salt and pepper, and lightly whisk them together.

5   Add the eggs to the béchamel sauce and whisk well until completely smooth. Add the Minas cheese and broccoli and fold everything together with a rubber spatula.

6   Pour the batter inside the prepared ramekins, about three quarters full. Sprinkle the Parmesan on top of each. Place the ramekins on a baking sheet and bake until they are puffed and lightly golden brown, 15 to 20 minutes.

7   Remove them from the oven and serve immediately.

TOASTED MANIOC FLOUR WITH EGGS AND SCALLIONS

Farofa de Ovo e Cebolinha

Farofa is the term for a side dish using toasted *farinha de mandioca*—in English, manioc flour, which is a dried flour similar in looks and texture to breadcrumbs, made from yucca (see the Glossary on page 170). The making of *farofa* as a dish couldn't be easier. It is plain manioc flour toasted in butter. A few of the classic *farofa* dishes include eggs and scallions, eggs and bacon, banana, bell peppers, and dendê oil, green beans and carrots, peas and corn, and so on and so forth. *Farofa* can be extremely dry, since the manioc flour immediately sucks up all the juices from anything it encounters, especially when it's served plain. The trick to making a moist *farofa* is to use a small amount of manioc flour in proportion to the other components, turning a side dish into a savory accompaniment that is so tempting, you may even forget there is a main course.

MAKES 4 SERVINGS

2 tablespoons unsalted butter
1½ cups manioc flour
2 tablespoons extra virgin olive oil
4 scallions (white and green parts), thinly
  sliced on a bias
5 large eggs
kosher salt and freshly ground black pepper

1 Melt the butter in a medium saucepan over low heat. Add the manioc flour and toast it to a light golden color, stirring often, 8 to 10 minutes. Make sure to stir constantly, otherwise the flour will burn. Set aside.

2 In a nonstick skillet, warm the olive oil over medium heat, and cook the scallions until they just start to soften. Save a few slices of scallion for garnish.

3 Whisk the eggs in a small bowl and season with salt and pepper. Pour the eggs into the scallions and scramble them lightly, being careful not to overcook them. Add the toasted manioc flour and stir everything together. Season with salt and pepper.

4 Pour into a serving dish and garnish with the reserved scallions.

Desserts
Sobremesas

CHOCOLATE BRIGADEIROS

Brigadeiro de Chocolate

Chewy, fudgy, addictive. These little choco-late fudge balls are as common and as loved in Brazil as cookies and brownies are in the United States. Traditionally, *brigadeiros* are a simple mixture of condensed milk, sweetened cocoa powder, and butter, cooked to a fudge state, then formed into little balls and rolled in chocolate sprinkles. I find this to be much too sweet, so I made a few changes to the original recipe, adding real chocolate, real cocoa pow-der, heavy cream, and corn syrup. Chocolate sprinkles are usually made with vegetable fat, so unless I know the sprinkle is made with real chocolate like the ones from Guittard or Cocoa Barry, I prefer to use cocoa powder, or grated chocolate, for rolling and the result is amazing. This is a perfect dessert to give as a gift for any occasion. Children will love it and so will adults.

MAKES ABOUT 45 BRIGADERIOS

2 (14-ounce) cans sweetened condensed milk

4 tablespoons unsalted butter

2 tablespoons heavy cream

2 teaspoons light corn syrup

3 ounces semisweet chocolate, chopped

2 teaspoons unsweetened cocoa powder

1 cup chocolate sprinkles, preferably Guittard

---

1   In a medium heavy-bottomed saucepan, place the condensed milk, butter, heavy cream, and corn syrup and bring to a boil over medium heat.

2   When the mixture starts to bubble, add the chocolate and the cocoa powder. Whisk well, making sure there are no pockets of cocoa powder. Reduce the heat to low and cook, whisking constantly, until it is the consisten-cy of a dense fudgy batter, 8 to 10 minutes. You want the mixture to bubble toward the end, so it's important to use low heat or the sides of the pan will burn the fudge. If you undercook it, the *brigadeiro* will be too soft; if you overcook it, it will be too chewy. It is done when you swirl the pan and the mixture slides as one soft piece, leaving a thick burnt residue on the bottom.

3   Slide the mixture into a bowl (without scrap-ing the bottom) and let cool at room temper-ature. Cover the bowl with plastic wrap and chill in the refrigerator for at least 4 hours.

4   Scoop the mixture by the teaspoonful and, using your hands, roll each into a little ball about ¾ inch in diameter (about the size of a chocolate truffle).

5   Place the sprinkles in a bowl. Roll 4 to 6 *brigadeiros* at a time through the sprinkles, making sure they cover the entire surface. Store in an airtight plastic container for 2 days or up to 1 month in the refrigerator.

COCONUT BRIGADEIROS
Brigadeiro de Côco

MAKES ABOUT 30 BRIGADERIOS

1 cup sweetened condensed milk
½ cup coconut milk
2 teaspoons light corn syrup
2 tablespoons unsalted butter
1½ cups unsweetened shredded coconut

Here's another version that I love and often catch myself sneaking in the kitchen at night to eat another one. Or two. Or six. If you can't find shredded coconut, buy flaked coconut or coconut chips and shred them in a food processor or grate them on the smallest hole of a grater. Be sure you buy unsweetened coconut, or else this recipe will be much too sweet.

1 In a medium heavy-bottomed saucepan, place the condensed milk, coconut milk, corn syrup, butter, and ½ cup of the shredded coconut. Bring to a boil over medium heat.

2 Reduce the heat to low and whisk constantly until the mixture is the consistency of a dense fudgy batter, 8 to 10 minutes. You want the mixture to bubble, so it's important to use low heat or else the sides of the pan will burn the coconut fudge. You know it is done when you swirl the pan around and the whole mixture slides as one soft piece, leaving burnt residue on the bottom of the pan.

3 Slide the mixture into a bowl (without scraping the bottom of the pan) and let cool at room temperature. Cover with plastic wrap and refrigerate for at least 4 hours.

4 Scoop the mixture by the teaspoonful and, using your hands, roll each into a little ball, ¾ inch in diameter.

5 Place the remaining 1 cup of shredded coconut in a bowl. Roll 4 to 6 *brigadeiros* at a time through the coconut, making sure it sticks and covers the entire outside surface. Store in an airtight plastic container at room temperature for 2 days or up to 1 month in the refrigerator. Make sure to eat them at room temperature.

ORIGINS OF A NAME:

The name "brigadeiro" comes from a Brazilian political figure, a brigadier named Eduardo Gomes, who in the early 1900s was admired for his good looks and who notoriously loved chocolate. When sweetened condensed milk was invented in Switzerland and brought to Brazil, cooks created this fudge using the sweet milk and chocolate. Legend has it that he liked it so much, the *brigadeiro* was named in his honor. Today, it is a standard in cafés, snack bars, and restaurants all over the country.

PISTACHIO BRIGADEIROS
Brigadeiro de Pistache

As you can tell, it becomes addictive exploring new variations of this popular candy. I love using pistachios for their beautiful color and nutty taste. Fabri is an Italian brand of pistachio paste available at www.muscofood.com. Like all *brigadeiros* recipes, call all kids in the house to help.

MAKES ABOUT 30 BRIGADERIOS

⅔ cup sweetened condensed milk

⅓ cup heavy cream

1 teaspoon light corn syrup

1 to 2 tablespoons pistachio paste

1 teaspoon unsalted butter

1 cup finely ground pistachios

1 Place the condensed milk, heavy cream, corn syrup, pistachio paste, and butter in a medium saucepan and bring to a boil over medium heat.

2 As soon as it starts to boil, turn the heat to low, and cook, whisking constantly, while the milk thickens into a dense fudge, 8 to 10 minutes. You know it is done when you tilt the pan and the whole fudge slides as a batter, leaving the burnt bits on the bottom of the pan.

3 Slide the mixture into a bowl (without scraping the bottom of the pan). Let cool at room temperature. Cover the bowl with plastic wrap and refrigerate for at least 4 hours.

4 Scoop the mixture by the teaspoonful and, using your hands, roll each into a little ball, ¾ inch in diameter.

5 Place the ground pistachios in a bowl. Roll 4 to 6 *brigadeiros* at a time in the nuts, making sure they cover the entire surface. Store in an airtight plastic container at room temperature for 2 days or up to 1 month in the refrigerator. Make sure to eat them at room temperature.

MOLTON DULCE DE LECHE CAKE

Bolinho Quente de Doce de Leite

I first tasted this variation of a chocolate molten cake at Carla Pernamburo's restaurant, Carlota. Dulce de leche is now available at most supermarkets and I used the canned Nestlé brand when developing this recipe—and was quite happy with the result. The idea to serve this cake alongside sour cream sorbet came from the typical Brazilian pairing of dulce de leche with cheese. The contrast of sweet and tangy, hot and cold, turned this dessert into one of my all-time favorites. If you want to serve it with vanilla ice cream it will still be incredible. But you must try this combination and I guarantee you will devour every bite of it.

MAKES 4 SERVINGS

8 tablespoons (1 stick) butter, plus extra for foil cups

1 cup dulce de leche, at room temperature

2 large egg yolks

2 large eggs

2 tablespoons sugar

⅛ teaspoon salt

¼ teaspoon ground cinnamon

1 teaspoon vanilla extract

¼ cup all-purpose flour, sifted, plus extra for foil cups

4 six-ounce foil cups

1 Preheat the oven to 350°F. Using a pastry brush, butter and flour 4 foil cups. Shake off the excess flour.

2 Melt the butter in a medium saucepan over very low heat. When the butter is just melted, remove the pan from the heat and add the dulce de leche. Whisk slowly and constantly until blended, 3 to 5 minutes.

3 In another bowl, whisk the yolks and whole eggs together. Add the sugar and salt. Pour the dulce de leche mixture into the eggs and whisk well. Add the cinnamon and vanilla and continue to whisk. Add the flour and fold gently with a rubber spatula, making sure there are no lumps.

SOUR CREAM SORBET

Bring ¾ cup water, 1 cup sugar, 2 tablespoons light corn syrup, and 1 tablespoon lemon zest to a boil. Strain directly into an ice bath and let cool completely. Whisk in 1 pound sour cream. Add 1 to 2 tablespoons lemon juice to taste and chill for 6 hours. Run through an ice cream machine, according to its instructions. Makes 1 quart.

4 Carefully pour the batter into the foil cups, filling each one almost to the top. (This can be done up to 5 days ahead and left in the refrigerator.) Bake the cakes until the edges are set but the center is still soft, about 6 to 8 minutes. (Be aware that the cake will not change much of its color during the baking time, nor will it rise.) Remember each oven is different and this is a delicate recipe. It's more important that you know what to look for than to rely on the exact minute amount.

5 Remove the cakes from the oven. Immediately invert each foil cup onto a plate and serve with a scoop of sour cream sorbet.

AVOCADO CRÈME BRÛLÉE

Crème Brûlée de Abacate

Most Americans think of only guacamole, salads, and maybe the adventurous hamburger when it comes to avocado. I really love to use avocados in desserts, the way we do in Brazil. The buttery texture of avocado lends a perfect creaminess to this reinvented crème brûlée, which unlike the classic recipe, is not baked at all. This mixture of avocado and condensed milk is simply puréed in a food processor. After you have simulated the consistency of a custard, you add a crunchy layer of burnt sugar on top immediately before serving. The result is a truly inspired dessert that takes less than five minutes to make plus a little chilling time. Because of its richness, this dessert can also act as a mini crème brûlée: Simply serve it in smaller ramekins. This will yield more servings, of course, depending on how small a ramekin you use.

FINDING BLOWTORCHES

Because crème brûlée has become so popular, it is very easy to find blowtorches these days. If there are no high-end kitchen stores near you, most hardware stores carry them. However, if you can't find one, you can use a broiler. Preheat the broiler and place the ramekins in an ice bath in a roasting pan. Spread the sugar as described in the recipe, and place the pan in the broiler. Depending on your broiler, it can take seconds or minutes to caramelize the sugar, so stand by watching very carefully. When the sugar starts to bubble remove the roasting pan from the broiler, then remove the ramekins from the ice bath.

MAKES 4 SERVINGS

1 cup sweetened condensed milk
2 medium firm-ripe Hass avocados, peeled, pitted, and cut into chunks
2 to 3 tablespoons fresh lemon juice
½ cup sugar, for topping

propane blowtorch
4 four-ounce ramekins

1   Place the condensed milk and avocados into a food processor and process until the mixture is velvety smooth, 1 to 2 minutes. Add the lemon juice 1 tablespoon at a time, and pulse for a few more seconds after each addition. At this point, taste the avocado cream to check if the lemon juice is giving the right balance. I usually use 2 tablespoons of fresh lemon juice and add a drop or two more, if necessary.

2   Using a rubber spatula, scrape the mixture into four ramekins, making sure it is nice and flat inside the ramekin. Chill for 4 hours in the refrigerator.

3   Right before serving, spread a thin layer of sugar evenly over the top of each custard. Ignite the torch to medium. Melt the sugar by moving the flame back and forth across the custard while maintaining a distance of 2 inches between the flame and the surface. The sugar will melt, bubble, then turn into a golden caramel. In less than a minute, it will harden to a delicious crust. Allow to cool for 3 to 5 minutes before serving. Do not brûlée the dessert more than 20 minutes in advance of serving.

BRAZILIAN CRÈME CARAMEL

Pudim de Leite

Almost every cuisine has its version of flan, but what makes the Brazilian take so special is the use of sweetened condensed milk, lending a smooth, silky, and velvety texture to the dish. In the traditional recipe, only milk is used, but I add a bit of heavy cream and extra yolks to expand upon the velvety texture that I like so much. As easy a recipe as flan is, I often see them baked too long or perforated with unsightly holes. With this recipe, the result is an entire spoonful of luxuriously smooth custard, with a caramel sauce oozing its way into every bite. You can prepare the dessert up to 5 days ahead of time, but only invert it the day you are serving it.

MAKES 6 TO 8 SERVINGS

¾ cup sugar
3 tablespoons water

1 14-ounce can sweetened condensed milk
1⅔ cups whole milk
½ cup heavy cream
3 large eggs
2 large egg yolks
1 teaspoon vanilla extract

8 x 2 round cake mold (or 4 6-ounce ramekins)

1   Preheat the oven to 350°F.

2   Place the sugar and water in a heavy-bottomed saucepan. Cook the sugar over high heat without stirring, until it turns into an amber-colored caramel, about 5 minutes. Pour the caramel into the cake mold and swirl around making sure the caramel evenly covers the whole bottom. You don't want to have any concentrated lumps of caramel in any part of the pan. Be advised that the caramel will continue to cook once it's off the heat, so work fast. Set the pan aside.

3   Mix all the ingredients for the flan in a food processor, until smooth. Slowly pour it into the prepared caramel mold. Transfer the mold to a large roasting pan and fill the pan with warm water so that it comes halfway up the sides of the mold. Place the roasting pan in the center of the oven and bake until the custard is set, 45 to 55 minutes.

4   Cool the mold on a wire rack, then refrigerate for at least 4 hours. It's important to invert the flan only when it is chilled completely, otherwise it might break.

5   Before serving, run a smooth knife around the inside of the mold. Place a large rimmed platter on top and, holding the dishes together with both hands, quickly invert the flan onto the platter. Hold for a minute to ensure all the caramel drips onto the platter.

PORTUGUESE STYLE ALMOND CAKE

Toucinho do Céu

Like many other recipes inherited from Portugal, the origin of Toucinho do Céu goes back hundreds of years to the convents where nuns used to cook sweets based on eggs and sugar and prepare recipes such as *pão de ló* (genoise cake), flans, and custards. Toucinho do Céu translates into "bacon-from-heaven," thanks to the traditional version of this recipe being made with pork lard. This lighter version has as much flavor without the fat. Unlike most almond cakes, which start with a creamy batter, this cake is prepared by cooking ground almonds in a simple syrup. The result is a very moist almond cake. While this makes a great snack, it's especially good as a dessert when paired with rhubarb and strawberry compote and some sweetened crème fraîche. It can also travel well when made in a bar form such as brownies.

MAKES 6 TO 8 SERVINGS

½ cup water

1¼ cups sugar

⅛ teaspoon salt

1¾ cups ground almonds, skinless

4 tablespoons unsalted butter, at room temperature, plus extra for greasing the pan

5 large egg yolks

2 large eggs

1 teaspoon almond extract (or Amaretto)

1 teaspoon orange zest, finely grated

all-purpose flour, for dusting

8 x 2 round cake mold

1 Preheat the oven to 325°F. Line the cake mold with parchment paper. Grease with butter and dust lightly with flour.

2 Bring the water, sugar, and salt to a boil in a big saucepan. Add the ground almonds. Stir gently but constantly over medium-low heat, until the mixture starts to thicken and you can see the bottom of the pan by stirring, about 2 minutes. Remove the pan from the heat and add the butter. Mix until the butter is melted and blended well.

3 In a medium bowl, lightly whisk the yolks and eggs, then mix into the almond mixture with a spatula. Add the almond extract and orange zest and stir well.

4 Pour the batter into the prepared mold. Bake until the cake is firm in the center and the top is lightly golden brown, 28 to 30 minutes. (If you overbake it, the cake becomes chewy.) Cool on a wire rack.

5 Invert the cake onto a platter (see opposite for technique). Lift off the pan, peel off the parchment paper, and cut the cake into wedges. Serve at room temperature.

COCONUT CUSTARD CAKE

Quindins

The Portuguese deserve all the credit for the love of sweets in Brazil. The African and indigenous heritages contributed more to the ingredients that were then incorporated into Portuguese sweets. For instance, *quindins* were developed by African women to please the Portuguese palate. It is a firm custard made from simple ingredients with an incredibly silky texture resulting from the slow-cooked egg yolks. The lime juice is a crucial ingredient to balance the sweetness. I owe many thanks to Carlos Coelho, the owner of a store that specializes in Brazilian ingredients in Bridgeport, Connecticut. Once, he took me to the kitchen just when the cook was preparing *quindins*. Of all the *quindins* I have tried in my life, this little but complete store offered my favorite version, which is adapted here.

MAKES 8 TO 10 SERVINGS

14 large egg yolks

1 large egg

1 cup sugar, plus more for dusting

⅛ teaspoon salt

⅓ cup, plus 2 tablespoons whole milk

¾ cup unsweetened finely shredded coconut

1 teaspoon fresh lime juice

butter, softened, for greasing

8- to 10-cavity muffin pan

1   Preheat the oven to 325°F. Butter the sides and bottoms of each muffin cavity and dust the insides with sugar. Shake off the excess and set them aside.

2   In a medium bowl, whisk the yolks, egg, sugar, and salt, until they are blended and slightly thickened. Add the milk and whisk well. Add the coconut and lime juice, then fold in everything with a rubber spatula.

3   Pour the batter into the prepared muffin pan, filling each cavity close to the top, but leaving about ¼-inch space to the edge. Set the muffin pan inside the roasting pan, in the preheated oven. After placing the roasting pan on the oven rack, pour 4 to 6 cups of warm water into the roasting pan under the muffin pan (or you can do this on the coun

ter, just be careful not to let any water drop into the batter when moving the roasting pan). This process is crucial to give this cake the right texture.

4   Bake until the custard is set and the top is lightly golden brown, 35 to 40 minutes. While in the oven, the coconut will rise to the top and create a crust; it can easily become too chewy if overcooked since it is the only part not receiving protection from the water bath, so remove the roasting pan from the oven as soon as it turns golden brown.

5   Cool the muffin pan on a wire rack for 20 to 30 minutes.

6   To unmold the *quindins*, run a small paring knife between the pan and each cake; each quindim should rotate inside the mold as you run the knife—that's a sign that it is cooked just right. Carefully invert the muffin pan to let all the *quindins* out. Give the pan a sharp tap, and the cake should unmold easily. If it doesn't, flip the pan back over and place it on a low burner for just a few seconds to melt the butter under the cakes.

7   Serve slightly chilled. You can prepare the *quindims* up to 5 days ahead of time and keep them in an airtight plastic container in the refrigerator.

GUAVA PASTE SOUFFLÉ WITH MASCARPONE SAUCE

Soufle de Goiabada com Calda de Mascarpone

This dish tells you a lot about what kind of restaurant Carlota is: contemporary Brazilian cooking. The cuisine of Carla Pernambuco, its chef and owner, playful and intelligent. One of her classic creations is a *Soufle de Goiabada com Calda de Catupiry*. It's a dish that translates the essence of Brazilian tradition to style and creativity. In my American kitchen, I adapted the recipe using mascarpone instead of catupiry cheese because it's easier to find and the result is simply fantastic. Unlike most soufflés that deflate within minutes out of the oven, this one is a bit more forgiving, giving you about 10 minutes, but like every other soufflé you should whip the egg whites just before baking. When working with fruit, it is natural to have taste variations due to ripeness, time of harvest, sugar, and pectin in the fruit. Different brands of guava paste, for example, present different consistencies, and you might need to adjust with more or less water to dissolve it. When I use the Fugini brand from Brazil, I only need ½ cup water. When I use the Goya brand, I need about 1¼ cups water.

MAKES 8 SERVINGS

FOR THE MASCARPONE SAUCE

1 cup heavy cream
1 tablespoon sugar
1 vanilla bean, scraped (see box on page 155)
1 cup mascarpone cheese

1¼ pounds guava paste
1 teaspoon fresh lemon juice
8 egg whites
⅛ teaspoon salt
1½ tablespoons sugar
butter and sugar, for greasing
confectioners' sugar, for dusting

8 six-ounce molds

1. In a medium saucepan, place the heavy cream, sugar, vanilla bean and its seeds and bring to a boil, whisking well to dissolve the sugar. Reduce the heat to low, add the cheese and whisk slowly, making sure the cheese is melting into the sauce. Remove the vanilla pod and pour the sauce into a serving bowl. This sauce can be done up to 3 days ahead of time and kept in an airtight plastic container in the refrigerator. To reheat, warm gently over low heat and whisk occasionally.

2. Preheat the oven to 350°F. Grease the molds with a thick coat of butter and sprinkle with sugar, tapping out the excess.

3　Cut the guava paste into small chunks, and place them in a medium saucepan. Add about ½ cup of water (more or less may be necessary). Cook over low heat, whisking constantly, until the paste melts. You are looking for a thick and pasty sauce without too much liquid. Remove from the heat.

4　Add the lemon juice and whisk well. Transfer the guava paste to a bowl and let it cool to room temperature, about 20 minutes. This step can be done up to 5 days ahead, and kept in an airtight plastic container in the refrigerator (just make sure to bring it to room temperature before mixing with the egg whites).

5　Working in a clean, dry bowl of an electric mixer fitted with the whisk attachment, whip the egg whites with the salt until they just turn opaque, gradually increasing the speed from medium to high.

6　Still beating, add the sugar in a slow steady stream and continue to beat until the peaks are firm and shiny. Using a large rubber spatula, fold one quarter of the egg whites into the guava paste. Gently fold in the remaining egg whites, making sure the batter is well folded, without any lumps.

7　Delicately turn the batter into the prepared mold. I like to use a pastry bag without a tip for this task, but a plain ladle will also work. Fill the ramekins almost to the top and place the molds on a baking sheet. Bake the soufflé in the oven until the top becomes lightly brown, about 12 minutes.

8　Remove the soufflés from the oven, and dust them with the confectioners' sugar. To serve, poke a hole in the center of each soufflé and pour some sauce inside.

PASSION FRUIT CANNOLI

Cannoli de Maracujá

Cannoli is one of my favorite Italian pastries. The classic Italian version has a crisp tubular shell filled with a creamy ricotta flavored with candied fruit. The Americanized version, which uses chocolate chips, has already become the new classic. Instead of using milk, I use coconut milk and passion fruit to lend a delicious mix of exotic and tropical flavors. These are not the easiest tuiles to work with because they harden quite fast. You have to spread it thin enough for a delicate cannoli, but not so thin that it breaks. Another option for presentation is to keep the tuiles flat and build a napoleon as opposed to a cannoli. Either way, this dessert is quite easy to do at home because everything is prepared ahead of time. But assembling must be done just before serving. If you want to get a little fancy, garnish wth some fresh berries and a cilantro syrup (see box opposite).

MAKES ABOUT 25 CANNOLI

FOR THE PASTRY CREAM
1 ⅔ cups coconut milk, plus 1 tablespoon
⅓ cup passion fruit juice, from concentrate
6 large egg yolks
⅓ cup sugar
¼ cup cornstarch

FOR THE TUILE
¾ cup toasted almonds
¼ cup unsweetened grated coconut
1 tablespoon all-purpose flour
1 tablespoon cocoa powder
2 tablespoons coconut milk
2 tablespoons light corn syrup
¼ cup sugar
5 tablespoons unsalted butter

6 to 8 cannoli tubes

1   Make the pastry cream. In a medium saucepan, bring the coconut milk and passion fruit juice to a boil over medium heat.

2   In a bowl, whisk together the yolks and sugar. Add the cornstarch and whisk until blended. Whisking all the while, pour about a quarter of the hot liquid into the yolk mixture. Still whisking, add the remaining hot liquid

to the yolks. Whisk well and transfer this mixture back to the saucepan.

3   Place the saucepan over medium-low heat and cook, whisking vigorously, until the cream starts to thicken and turns from liquid into a creamy consistency, about 5 minutes.

4   Cover a sheet pan with a layer of plastic wrap and pour the cream onto it. Spread into

a thin layer and cool to room temperature. Cover with plastic wrap and refrigerate for at least 2 hours or up to 2 days.

5   Meanwhile make the tuiles. In the bowl of a food processor, grind the almonds and coconut until they become a fine powder, about 1 minute. Add the flour and cocoa powder and process until it's well blended. Transfer to a bowl and set aside.

6   In a medium saucepan, bring the coconut milk, corn syrup, sugar, and butter to a boil. Reduce the heat to low and cook until the mixture bubbles vigorously, about 3 minutes. Remove the pan from the heat and add the almond-coconut mixture. Fold together with a rubber spatula until well blended.

7   At this point you have to work relatively fast or else the batter might harden. Split the batter in half and spread each half onto a 12 x 18 baking sheet lined with parchment paper. Cover each sheet with another sheet of parchment paper. Using a rolling pin, roll a thin layer, spreading the batter to fit the sheet. Chill in the refrigerator until the tuiles harden, about 2 hours.

8   Preheat the oven to 350°F. Remove the tuiles from the refrigerator. Using a 3-inch round cookie cutter, cut 10 to 12 circles of tuile per baking sheet. Line a baking sheet with parchment paper and place 6 tuiles on it, leaving at least 3 inches of space between each tuile. (You can store sheets of parchment paper lined with circles of tuiles in the refrigerator for up to 5 days or in the freezer for up to a month.

9   Bake the tuiles in the oven until they bubble and look done, about 8 minutes. Immediately remove the baking sheet from the oven and, using a flat offset spatula, flip each circle upside down so that the textured side faces out. Roll around a cannoli tube (don't roll it too tight or it may be difficult to remove the metal tube from inside the tuile), being careful not to burn your fingers. Let each rolled tuille harden around the cannoli tube for at least 2 minutes to maintain its round shape before pushing the tube out. If while you are rolling some tuiles, others gets hard, reheat them in the oven for another minute before rolling. Repeat with all the batter.

10   Remove the cream from the refrigerator at least 30 minutes before assembling. Beat in the bowl of an electric mixer fitted with the paddle attachment at medium speed to lighten up the cream. Place the pastry cream in a pastry bag or a ziplock bag. Cut a small opening and carefully pipe into both ends of the cannoli.

MAKING SYRUP

When I was working in restaurant pastry kitchens, I learned that chefs like to keep some herb syrups (such as cilantro, mint, or basil) to use as garnishes. It's quite easy to make one: Plunge about ½ cup of packed herbs into boiling water for 15 seconds, drain and plunge into an iced water bath. Remove the herbs from the water and combine them in a blender or food processor with ⅔ cup of corn syrup. Blend, strain, and discard the solids. The syrup will keep fresh, covered in the refrigerator, for 1 to 2 days.

COFFEE SOUFFLÉ WITH DULCE DE LECHE SAUCE

Soufflé de Café com Calda de Doce de Leite

Coffee is one of Brazil's most important commodities and I was itching to make a dessert using such a traditional Brazilian flavor. I tried it in mousses, custards, and parfaits. But there is something about a hot soufflé that brings you closer to the sensation of drinking a cup of strong, freshly brewed coffee. The sweetness of the dulce de leche sauce complements the flavor of coffee and adds a velvety taste to the airy texture of a soufflé.

MAKES 6 SERVINGS

1½ cups milk
4 teaspoons instant espresso coffee powder
5 large egg yolks
⅓ cup sugar
1 tablespoon, plus 2 teaspoons flour
1 tablespoon, plus 2 teaspoons cornstarch

8 egg whites
pinch of salt
3 tablespoons sugar
confectioners' sugar, for dusting
Dulce de Leche Sauce (recipe follows)

6 six-ounce ramekins, greased and sugared

1   Preheat the oven to 350°F. In a medium saucepan, bring the milk to a boil. Turn off the heat and whisk in the instant coffee.

2   In a separate bowl, whisk together the egg yolks with sugar until yellow and pale.

3   Sift together the flour and cornstarch and add to the egg yolks, whisking until there are no lumps. Carefully pour in the hot milk, always whisking well. Transfer back to the saucepan and cook over low heat, whisking constantly, until it thickens, about 4 minutes. Transfer to a bowl and let cool.

4   In the bowl of an electric mixer fitted with the whisk attachment, beat the egg whites with a pinch of salt until they foam and rise. Gradually add the sugar and beat at medium-high speed until glossy soft peaks form.

5   Using a large spatula, fold one quarter of the whites into the pastry cream to lighten it, then gently fold in the remaining whites. Pour the soufflé batter into the ramekins, three quarters full. Place on a baking sheet and bake until they are puffed and golden brown, 15 to 18 minutes.

6   Remove from the oven and dust with confectioners' sugar. Poke a hole in the center of each soufflé and pour some warm Dulce de Leche Sauce in. Serve immediately.

HOT DULCE DE LECHE SAUCE

Calda de Doce de Leite

This recipe is incredibly easy to make and serves many purposes. I like to use it not only as a sauce for soufflés but also for ice cream toppings, in crepes, and with many other desserts. It is versatile: spreadable when cold and pourable when warm.

MAKES 2 CUPS

1 cup milk
½ cup heavy cream
2 tablespoons unsalted butter
1 cup dulce de leche, store bought,
   at room temperature

1. In a heavy-bottomed saucepan, combine the milk, heavy cream, and butter and bring to a boil over high heat. Boil for 1 minute and remove the pan from the heat.

2. Add the dulce de leche and whisk gently but constantly in ever-widening circles.

3. When smooth, return the saucepan to the stove, and cook over high heat, whisking constantly, until you reach a full boil. Reduce the heat to medium and cook, still whisking, until the sauce becomes thick and creamy, 3 to 5 minutes.

4. If you want to use the sauce in its pourable state, let it cool for about 10 minutes. If you want to save it for later, keep it in a plastic container covered with a tight-fitting lid for at least 2 weeks in the refrigerator (reheat in a saucepan over low heat, whisking constantly, or in the microwave, 10 seconds at a time, whisking after each turn, until it's hot and pourable).

FIG TERRINE WITH DULCE DE LECHE SAUCE

Terrine de Figos com Calda de Doce de Leite e Avelas

This dessert is based on a method I learned from a caterer in Rio when I was 15. Demar is known for his perfect fig desserts and when I asked him how he prepared them, he explained that when figs are peeled and packed together, they stick to one another as if they are one large fruit. I have been using that little trick for years. Here, I use a loaf pan, so I had to use lots of figs to fill it up. But you can use any size mold or even a small round cake pan, as long as you pack it full. The pairing of the cold molded fruit with the warm Dulce de Leche Sauce makes this dessert a decadent experience of taste, temperature, and texture—not to mention a beautiful presentation. Unmolding this terrine is a glorious unveiling that should be done in front of your guests. Garnish with toasted and chopped hazelnuts for crunch.

MAKES 8 SERVINGS

2½ pounds figs, about 40 figs
Dulce de Leche Sauce (page 149)

9 x 3 x 3 loaf pan

BUYING FIGS

There are three types of figs: Black Mission, Kadota, and Brown Turkey. They all can be used for this recipe because the difference in taste is very slim. However, don't mix the varieties because the color of the terrine will be unharmonious. Figs are quite perishable, so I would recommend preparing the terrine not more than 1 or 2 days before serving. Try to choose figs that are not too green or too ripe. If you press the fruit with your thumb it should feel slightly soft.

1 Line the loaf pan with plastic wrap, making sure the plastic is touching the walls and the bottom of the pan (spritz the pan with a little water, this helps the plastic wrap stick to it). Use more than enough wrap to line the pan as you'll need excess to seal the top of it after the figs are packed in.

2 Cut off the top stems, then peel and cut all the figs in half. Arrange the figs inside the pan, with their centers facing out, lightly pressing them together and making sure there is minimal space between each fig. Seal the pan with the extra plastic wrap and place it, open side up, in the refrigerator to chill overnight.

3 When it is time to serve, open the plastic wrap, place the terrine facing down on a rectangular plate or a cutting board, and lift off the loaf pan. Peel off the plastic wrap and, using a serrated knife, cut slices about 1 inch thick and place each one on a plate. The slices on the ends won't look as pretty and won't hold as well as the rest of the slices in the center. Remember that there is nothing holding the figs other than Mother Nature so make sure to aim for a 1-inch thickness or the figs will fall apart.

4 Pour warm Dulce de Leche Sauce on top of each slice.

CHURROS

For me, churros are a work of art. Not a fancy-food work of art, but street-food work of art. And I am so happy that they have emigrated across America. This recipe is based on the churros I often eat at Praca Nossa Senhora da Paz in Ipanema. They are sold in carts that cluster the corners of Rio's streets; on weekends, they relocate to the vast stretches of our Atlantic beaches. Served in a small paper bag, you get crispy fried dough, dusted with cinnamon sugar, and filled from top to bottom with an injection of dulce de leche squirting out from the center and dripping into your fingers.

Unlike an American doughnut, the center remains pale, moist, and chewy. In looking to adapt this indulgent experience for our home kitchens, I bought the largest star tip I could find (about 1 inch in diameter on the opening), two pastry bags (one for the dough, one for the dulce de leche), and a tube tip (a pastry bag tip that has a thin 2-inch tube attached). The size of the star tip is key to the success of churros—if the star tip is not wide enough, the churros will be too thin and much too crunchy. I found the tools for making these churros at www.jbprince.com.

1 cup sugar

1 tablespoon ground cinnamon

1 cup all-purpose flour

1 teaspoon baking powder

1½ cups water

1 tablespoon olive oil

⅛ teaspoon salt

1 teaspoon sugar

2 quarts vegetable oil, for frying

1 can ready-made dulce de leche,
   at room temperature

ORIGINS OF CHURROS

Many churros recipes are based on fried pate a choux dough served with a chocolate sauce. I don't think churros and chocolate make a good match, surprising coming from a chocoholic like me. In my opinion, the flavor of chocolate overwhelms the fried dough and the consistency of the sauce is too thin. In Brazil, we serve it filled with dulce de leche. The dough is also different, based on flour and water only, no eggs at all; it is stiff enough to be shaped, but also moist enough to retain some sponginess.

1 In a shallow bowl, combine the sugar and cinnamon and mix well. Set aside.

2 In a small bowl sift together the flour and baking powder.

3 In a medium saucepan, bring the water, olive oil, salt, and sugar to a boil. Add the flour all at once and mix vigorously until a dough forms and pulls away from the sides of the pan, about 30 seconds. The dough will look stiff and not very smooth.

4 Transfer the dough to a floured surface and let cool, about 10 minutes. Knead the dough lightly with your hands until it becomes a smooth ball.

5 Fill a medium pan with 2 inches of oil. Heat the oil to 350°F, as measured by a deep-fat frying thermometer.

6 Spoon the dough into a pastry bag fitted with the largest star tip you can find. Hold the pastry bag directly above the oil and press strips of dough 4 to 5 inches long, snipping

with your finger. Fry them in batches until lightly golden brown all over, 2 to 3 minutes.

7 Using a slotted spoon, transfer the dough to a flat plate lined with a double thickness of paper towels to absorb any extra oil. Let the churros dry for a minute and, while still hot, roll them in the cinnamon sugar mixture. (Churros can be done in advance and kept warm in a low temperature oven.)

8 Spoon the dulce de leche inside another pastry bag fitted with a tube tip and insert the tube in the center of each churro as far as it will go. Apply pressure to release the dulce de leche while slowly moving the tube tip out.

9 Serve with plenty of napkins.

COCONUT MOUSSE

Mousse de Côco

This classic Brazilian mousse is all about coconut. I like to serve it with a complementary sauce also based on coconut—Baba de Moça (see recipe opposite). Cloudy and airy, each bite is rich and refreshing with traces of coconut melting in your mouth. Fresh coconut shavings make the best garnish but lightly toasted dried coconut chips are just as wonderful. This mousse can be done up to 3 days ahead of time and kept in the refrigerator covered with plastic wrap.

MAKES 8 SERVINGS

1 (14-ounce) can sweetened condensed milk
1⅔ cups coconut milk
1 cup unsweetened dried grated coconut (see box on page 158)
2½ teaspoons (1 envelope) unflavored gelatin
½ cup heavy cream
4 egg whites
pinch of salt
1 tablespoon sugar
shaved coconut chips, lightly toasted, for garnish

1   In a medium bowl, whisk together the sweetened condensed milk, 1 cup coconut milk, and the dried coconut. Set aside.

2   In a small saucepan, place the remaining ⅔ cup coconut milk, sprinkle the gelatin on top, and give it a quick whisk. Let stand at room temperature for about 2 minutes. Bring to a bare simmer over very low heat, whisking gently, until the gelatin is dissolved (but do not let it boil), about 1 minute.

3   Pour the gelatin-coconut milk into the sweetened condensed mixture and whisk well. Let sit at room temperature for 10 minutes.

4   In the bowl of an electric mixer fitted with the whisk attachment, whip the heavy cream until it holds soft peaks, and then gently fold it into the coconut mixture. If you see any lumps, mix with a spatula to get rid of them.

5   In another clean bowl of an electric mixer fitted with the whisk attachment, beat the egg whites with a tiny pinch of salt. Start on low speed and gradually increase as the whites begin to foam and rise. Slowly add the sugar and beat until soft peaks form. Fold it gently into the coconut mixture, knowing that just like the whipped cream, the egg whites will become somewhat liquid once they are mixed into the base. Make sure there are no lumps.

6   Pour the coconut mousse into a nice glass bowl and cover with plastic wrap. Chill in the refrigerator until it's set, about 6 hours, preferably overnight.

7   To serve, garnish with some toasted coconut chips and Baba de Moça sauce.

COCONUT CUSTARD SAUCE

Baba de Moça

⅓ cup whole milk

1⅔ cups coconut milk

1 vanilla bean

6 large egg yolks

½ cup sugar

Based on egg yolks, coconut milk, and sugar, this classic sauce, when served by itself, was among my favorite childhood treats. Like a crème Anglaise, Baba de Moça is a very versatile sauce—I serve it with coconut mousse, chocolate cake, and many other desserts. I hope you will find many uses for this recipe, but don't feel guilty sampling it straight from the spoon.

1 In a medium saucepan, bring the milk, coconut milk, and scraped vanilla bean to a boil.

2 In a bowl, whisk together the egg yolks and sugar until the mixture becomes thick and pale yellow. Drizzle a little bit of the hot milk into the yolks to prevent them from curdling, then slowly pour in the remaining milk, whisking vigorously all the while.

3 Return the sauce to the saucepan and cook over low heat, stirring with a wooden spoon until the custard thickens and coats the back of the spoon.

4 Immediately remove the pan from the heat and strain the custard through a fine sieve and into a bowl. Discard the vanilla bean and place the bowl over an ice bath. When it is chilled, place the sauce in a plastic container covered with a tight-fitting lid and store it in the refrigerator. This sauce can be prepared up to 3 days ahead of serving.

VANILLA BEANS

The best vanilla beans come from Madagascar, Tahiti, and Mexico. When buying vanilla beans make sure they are soft and oily, not dry. A good vanilla bean should bend, not crack, when split in half. If it cracks, don't even bother using it because the bean is old and dry and the flavor is almost gone. Always store vanilla beans wrapped in a ziplock plastic bag in a dry place such as a pantry. Do not store vanilla beans in the refrigerator. To scrape a vanilla bean, slice it in half lengthwise with a sharp knife and use the blunt side of the knife to scrape out the pulp. Add both the pulp and the pod to the recipe. Many pastry chefs infuse their sugar with vanilla beans. To do so, simply air-dry a vanilla bean after use, then bury it in white granulated sugar and store it in an airtight jar. This is an easy way to add extra flavor to all of your desserts.

CHOCOLATE AND CUPUAÇÚ PUDDING

Copa de Chocolate e Cupuaçú

The scent of cupuaçu recalls the exotic perfumes of the Amazon. Cupuaçu's taste is quite hard to describe, but it falls somewhere between a banana and white chocolate, with an alcoholic tang at the end. It's a delicious reward for an exploratory palate. It's not hard to harness this unknown fruit into a delectable dessert. Simply make a pastry cream and add the fruit pulp at the end, then make a chocolate ganache to pour on top. It tastes like nothing you've ever tried before and it can be assembled up to 5 days before serving.

FOR THE CHOCOLATE CRUMBLE

⅓ cup all-purpose flour

1 tablespoon cornstarch

2 tablespoons cocoa powder

¼ cup almond flour

⅛ teaspoon salt

¼ cup, plus 2 tablespoons sugar

4 tablespoons unsalted butter, at room temperature

FOR THE CUPUAÇU LAYER

1 cup whole milk

3 large egg yolks

⅓ cup, plus 1 tablespoon sugar

1 tablespoon all-purpose flour, sifted

2 tablespoons cornstarch, sifted

⅔ cup cupuaçu pulp, thawed

FOR THE CHOCOLATE LAYER

½ pound semisweet chocolate

1¼ cups heavy cream

8 wineglasses or glass ramekins

1 Preheat the oven to 350°F.

2 In the bowl of an electric mixer fitted with the paddle attachment, mix all the chocolate crumble ingredients together until it resembles a coarse meal. Spread the mixture onto a baking sheet and bake until it dries, 12 to 14 minutes, rotating once. Remove from the oven and let cool. (You can prepare this up to 2 days ahead of time and keep it in an airtight plastic container at a cool and dry room temperature.)

3 Meanwhile, prepare the pastry cream. In a medium saucepan, heat the milk over medium heat.

4 In a medium bowl, whisk together the egg yolks and sugar until they become pale and yellow. Add the flour and cornstarch and whisk until blended and thick.

5 Gently drizzle some of the hot milk into the egg yolks to prevent curdling, then add the remaining milk. Transfer the mixture back to the saucepan, and cook over very low heat, whisking constantly (make sure to get into the edges of the pan), until it takes on a custard's consistency, 5 to 7 minutes. Immediately scrape the pastry cream into a bowl and, while it's still hot, whisk in the cupuaçú pulp. Cool at room temperature, stirring occasionally with a spatula.

6 Fill each glass with about ¼ cup of the cupuaçu cream. Chill in the refrigerator for at least 4 hours. Meanwhile, prepare the chocolate ganache. Chop the chocolate into small pieces and place it in a stainless-steel bowl.

7 In a small saucepan, bring the heavy cream to a boil and immediately pour it over the chocolate. Stir the mixture carefully with a rubber spatula starting from the center of the bowl, gradually incorporating the whole mixture until it's only just blended. Let cool at room temperature for 20 to 30 minutes, stirring occasionally with a spatula.

8 Transfer the ganache to a disposable pastry bag or ziplock bag with the corner cut. Carefully squeeze the chocolate ganache over the cupuaçú cream and tap the side of the glasses to make sure there are no pockets of air. Chill the glasses in the refrigerator for 3 hours or overnight.

9 Remove them from the refrigerator 30 minutes before serving. Garnish with the crumble.

COCONUT CHEESECAKE WITH GUAVA SAUCE

Cheesecake de Côco com Calda de Goiaba

GRATING COCONUT

The most practical form to buy coconut is dried, shredded, and unsweetened. If, however, you prefer to use a fresh coconut, you will need a hammer and a screwdriver to crack it open. Break it up into chunks and peel off the brown skin from the coconut meat. Grate it finely for the crust and shave it more coarsely for the garnish. If the coconut you buy is not fine enough, just pass it through the food processor. You can also toast the coconut chips. When you shave them, know that bigger is better. Place them in a 300°F oven until the chips start to get lightly golden brown, 3 to 5 minutes.

This is a Brazilian take on a classic American dessert. I changed the regular graham cracker crust to a chocolate one (simply run the crackers in the food processor until it's a fine crumble) and added coconut. It's very important to use unsweetened coconut, otherwise the crust will be sticky. The filling is a combination of Brazilian and American ingredients. It's deliciously creamy and sets up quite well in the presence of gelatin. The guava sauce complements the cheesecake in a classic Brazilian way, while still remaining somewhat close in flavor to the strawberry or cherry sauces often used in the States. I used the guava juice in concentrated form, but you can also use frozen guava pulp by omitting the cornstarch and cooking the pulp and sugar together until it thickens slightly.

FOR THE CRUST

1¼ cups chocolate graham crumbs

⅓ cup unsweetened finely grated coconut

1 teaspoon sugar

6 tablespoons unsalted butter, melted and cooled

FOR THE FILLING

2 teaspoons unflavored powdered gelatin

¾ cup coconut milk

½ cup cream cheese, softened

½ cup condensed milk

½ cup heavy cream

½ cup sour cream

1 tablespoon sugar

1 tablespoon Malibu rum

½ cup unsweetened grated coconut

FOR THE GUAVA SAUCE

1 tablespoon cornstarch

2 cups guava juice, from concentrate

¾ cup sugar

a few drops of fresh lemon juice

coconut chips, for garnish

10-inch fluted pie pan or 10-inch springform pan

1   Preheat the oven to 350°F.

2   In the bowl of a food processor or a mixer fitted with the paddle attachment, combine the graham crumbs, coconut, and sugar. Process until well combined, then slowly drizzle in the butter until the crumbs are uniformly moist. Using your hands, press the mixture into the pan, patting an even layer on the bottom and all the way up the sides. Bake for 10 to 12 minutes, then cool on a wire rack.

3   Meanwhile, prepare the filling. In a small saucepan, sprinkle the gelatin over the coconut milk and give it a whisk. Allow the gelatin to soften for 5 minutes.

4   In another medium saucepan, bring the cream cheese and condensed milk to a light simmer over medium heat. Whisk until smooth. Transfer to a bowl.

5   Over low heat, bring the gelatin and coconut milk to a low simmer, just until the gelatin melts. Do not let boil. Immediately pour into the cream cheese mixture, whisk well, and let everything cool to room temperature.

6   In the bowl of an electric mixer fitted with the whisk attachment, whip the heavy cream and sour cream together. Gradually add the sugar and beat until the mixture forms medium peaks. Gently fold the whipped cream with a rubber spatula into the cream cheese mixture. Add the rum and the grated coconut while folding. Pour the filling into the cooled crust and refrigerate until set, about 4 hours.

7   Meanwhile, prepare the guava sauce. In a small bowl, whisk the cornstarch with 3 tablespoons of the guava juice and set aside.

8   In a medium heavy-bottomed saucepan, bring the remaining guava juice and sugar to a simmer, whisking until hot. Add the cornstarch mixture and bring everything to a boil, whisking constantly, until the sauce has thickened to a syrup. Add a few drops of lemon juice to taste. Transfer to an airtight container and chill in the refrigerator. (The sauce can be done up to 3 days in advance.)

9   Remove the cheesecake from the refrigerator 20 to 30 minutes before serving. Garnish with toasted coconut chips and serve with the guava sauce drizzled on top.

PASSION FRUIT CREPES SOUFFLÉ

Crepes Soufflé de Maracujá

Claude Troisgros came to Rio in 1978. His father, Pierre, and his uncle, Jean, two of the most famous members of a generation of chefs who defined French cuisine, sealed the Troisgrois name. Claude brought to Rio all the honors of their legacy. He was a pioneer in working with Brazilian ingredients, a movement he created over 30 years ago, and he has been inspiring not only a new generation of Brazilian chefs but a new generation of discerning diners to care about their own Brazilian ingredients. This is one of his best recipes. The components of this dessert are as plain as can be. It's the way they are constructed that makes this recipe so special. The crepe is a crepe soufflé: the batter is suspended with egg whites and the crepe is cooked on one side only, in a pan, then baked in the oven until the edges are set. When it comes out of the oven, it is filled with a small amount of pastry cream. The crepe is then burned like a crème brûlée; however, it is very easy to burn—it's worth trying but powdered sugar can do the trick as well. This recipe can be done up to 5 days in advance and reheated before serving.

MAKES 10 TO 12 SERVINGS

FOR THE SAUCE

½ cup sugar

2 tablespoons water

1 cup passion fruit pulp, thawed

8 tablespoons (1 stick) unsalted butter, cold, cut into cubes

FOR THE CREPES

1 cup whole milk

3 tablespoons butter, more for cooking the crepes

5 eggs, separated

½ cup sugar (divided in half), plus more for dusting

⅓ cup, plus 2 tablespoons flour, sifted

pinch of salt

FOR THE PASTRY CREAM

See page 146 (Passion Fruit Cannoli)

1   In a medium saucepan, cook the sugar and water over high heat until the sugar turns into a light caramel color, 3 to 5 minutes. (You don't want a dark caramel for this sauce, or it will make the passion fruit sauce bitter.) Add the fruit pulp and cook, whisking constantly, over low heat for 3 to 5 minutes. Strain through a fine sieve and pour into another saucepan.

2   Place the saucepan over very low heat and add the cold pieces of butter, swirling the pan, until all the butter has melted. Don't let it boil. This sauce can be made up to 5 days

ahead of time; store it in a plastic container covered with a tight lid in the refrigerator.

3   Meanwhile, prepare the crepes. Preheat the oven to 375°F.

4   In a medium saucepan, bring the milk and butter to a gentle simmer over low heat.

5   In the bowl of an electric mixer fitted with the whisk attachment, mix the egg yolks and half of the sugar. Beat until the yolks turn yellow and pale, about 3 minutes. Turn the machine off and add the flour, whisking well by hand until blended.

6   Carefully pour some of the hot milk into the egg yolk mixture, then add the remaining milk. Whisk well by hand. At this point the batter should look creamy. Let cool at room temperature for at least 10 minutes.

7   In another bowl of an electric mixer fitted with the whisk attachment, place the egg whites with a pinch of salt and beat until they start to foam and rise. Gradually add the remaining sugar, turn the speed to medium-high, and beat until glossy soft peaks forms. Using a rubber spatula, fold one quarter of the egg whites into the yolk mixture, then gently fold in the remaining whites.

8   Heat an omelet pan over very low heat and melt the butter. Using a medium ladle (¾ to 1 cup), transfer one ladle of the crepe batter to the pan and using the back of the ladle, lightly spread the batter just to the rim of the pan—not up the sides. Cook the crepe over very low heat for 1 to 3 minutes. Check the bottom of the crepe by carefully lifting one side of the crepe. It should look nicely golden brown.

9   Immediately transfer the crepe to the oven for 3 to 5 minutes, until the edges of the crepe are very lightly golden brown (if your crepe pan is not ovenproof simply slide the crepe onto a baking sheet and place it in the oven). Don't let the center of the crepe get brown.

10   Slide the crepe onto the counter and while still hot (otherwise it won't seal) fill the crepe with 2 tablespoons of the filling and seal it by pinching the two edges tightly with your fingers. It should have the shape of a half moon and it should be puffed up in the center.

11   Repeat with all the crepe batter, making sure to wipe the omelet pan with a paper towel between each crepe. As each crepe is baked, filled, and closed, transfer them to a wire rack. You should have enough to make 10 to 12 crepes. This step can be done up to 5 days ahead and kept in a plastic container covered with a tight lid in the refrigerator.

12   To serve, place all the crepes on a baking sheet and heat them in a 350°F oven for 5 minutes. Gently warm the sauce over low heat, without letting it boil.

13   Remove the sheet from the oven and sprinkle a thin layer of sugar on each crepe, concentrating on the small, flattest area of the rounded crepe. Use a blowtorch to burn it, just as if you were burning a crème brûlée. You want to caramelize just the sugar, not the crepe dough.

14   Spoon the sauce equally onto individual plates and swirl to fit the circle shape of the plate. Transfer the caramelized crepe soufflé to the plate and serve immediately.

PEANUT BRITTLE

Pé de Moleque

Although you can use a variety of nuts, the brittle of my childhood is made with peanuts that are transformed into a munchy-crunchy caramel candy through the addition of sugar, butter, corn syrup, and honey. (I learned from master chef Jacques Torres that honey adds a great touch to brittles.) This is culinary alchemy at its best. I love to give brittle as a homemade gift. It can be eaten as a candy on its own or added as a crunchy element to ice cream. When making these candies, keep in mind that humidity will turn them sticky. The brittle keeps nice and crunchy in a cool and dry place. Be sure to keep the nuts halved or whole, not chopped.

MAKES ABOUT 1½ POUNDS

¾ cup sugar

1½ sticks (12 tablespoons) unsalted butter

1 teaspoon kosher salt

¼ cup light corn syrup

¼ cup honey

3 cups peanuts (whole, unsalted, and roasted)

1   In a large heavy-bottomed saucepan, place the sugar, butter, salt, corn syrup, and honey and melt over medium heat, stirring slowly with a wooden spoon for 2 to 3 minutes. As soon as the mixture reaches a pale yellow, add the peanuts and turn the heat to low.

2   Stirring constantly with a wooden spoon, roast the peanuts slowly until they start to turn a golden caramel color, 12 to 15 minutes. You know it's done when the peanuts start to smoke and you lift up the wooden spoon and they hold onto each other (as opposed to falling immediately off the spoon). Know that they continue to darken off of the heat.

3   Immediately pour the mixture onto a baking sheet lined with parchment paper. Cover with another layer of parchment paper and use a rolling pin to spread the brittle thin, trying to fit the baking sheet as best as you can. Be careful not to burn your hands.—you have to do this while it's very hot. Let the brittle cool completely at room temperature, then with your hands, break it into 2-inch pieces. Store in an airtight plastic container in a cool and dry place for up to 3 weeks.

PEANUT BUTTER TRUFFLES

Trufas de Paçoca

Paçoca is our version of peanut butter, though it is not puréed and spreadable; rather, the peanuts are ground with a little bit of manioc starch and sugar, then pressed, shaped, and wrapped as a candy. Americans and Brazilians both share not only a love for peanut treats but an affinity for adding chocolate to the mix. You can find *paçoca* in any Brazilian store, but finely chopped peanuts (with no skin) make a good substitute. If using peanut butter where the butter and the oil have separated, do not mix the oil back, simply pour it out and measure just the paste. When making this recipe, be sure to pay attention to one important detail: temperature (see box opposite). It affects both the filling and the chocolate coating. When forming the filling, the full batch can become too warm to hold a shape before you finish. To solve this problem, divide the batter into two batches before you chill it, and work with one at a time. If there is one way to make this recipe easier, it is to use top-quality chocolate, such as Valhrona, Guittard, Schaffer Berger, Callebeaut, or Michel Cluizel, because they all have a great amount of cocoa butter, which is the key to tempering chocolate.

MAKES ABOUT 50 TRUFFLES

7 ounces milk chocolate, chopped
1 cup crunchy roasted peanut butter
 (about ½ pound)
⅛ cup sugar
1 teaspoon kosher salt
3 tablespoons unsalted butter, at room
 temperature

12 paçocas (about 10 ounces)
½ pound bittersweet chocolate

1 Place the milk chocolate in a stainless-steel bowl and set it over a pot of simmering water. Make sure the bottom of the bowl doesn't touch the water. Melt the chocolate, stirring constantly with a rubber spatula. Before the chocolate is all melted, remove the bowl from the heat and stir it as it finishes melting—this prevents the chocolate from overheating. Let cool without allowing it to harden, about 15 minutes.

2 While the chocolate is cooling, place the peanut butter, sugar, and salt in the bowl of a food processor. Process for 3 to 5 minutes, making sure the sugar and salt are all dissolved in the peanut butter. Add the cooled chocolate and process until everything is well mixed. Add the butter and continue to process until the butter is all melted, about 2 more minutes.

TEMPERING CHOCOLATE

When making chocolate candy it's important to temper the chocolate. When you melt chocolate, you modify the molecules of fat and in order to make your chocolate nice and shiny again, you need to put the molecules of fat back together the right way—by tempering, or your chocolate will look grainy and stained. My favorite method of tempering chocolate is to add chopped chocolate to the melted chocolate. Many times chocolate is tempered the right way but still measures 92°–93°F on a candy thermometer. This means I have to wait a few more minutes until the temperature drops just a few more degrees (see below). On the other hand, letting the chocolate sit until it reaches the ideal working temperature is not the best way to do it because the fact that your chocolate is at the right temperature does not mean it was tempered the right way.

Without focusing on any brand, here are the ideal working temperatures for:

Dark chocolate, between 88°–91°F

Milk chocolate, between 84°–86°F

White chocolate, between 82°–84°F

3   Transfer the mixture equally to two plastic containers. Let cool to room temperature, then cover with a tight lid and place it in the refrigerator for at least 6 hours, preferably overnight. (The filling can be kept in the refrigerator for up to 2 weeks.)

4   Using a teaspoon, make little balls using the palm of your hands and place them on a flat baking sheet lined with parchment paper. Clean your hands often and work with half a batch at a time, keeping the other half cold in the refrigerator. Chill the balls in the refrigerator to set, about 30 minutes. Remove them from the refrigerator about 5 minutes before dipping them in the melted chocolate to avoid a shock of temperatures.

5   To make the coating, crumble the paçocas with your hands until it's a coarse powder and place it on a large gratin dish.

6   Melt two-thirds of the bittersweet chocolate in a metal bowl set over a pot of simmering water. Make sure the bottom of the bowl doesn't touch the water. Stir the chocolate with a spatula. As with the prior chocolate, remove the bowl from the heat before it is all melted and finish the melting by stirring it. Add the remaining one third of chopped chocolate to the bowl. Stir with a rubber spatula to melt the new chocolate into the already melted chocolate and leave it at room temperature for about 10 minutes.

7   Organize your working space with the tray of truffles on your left, the melted chocolate in the middle, and the crumbled paçoca on your right. Using a chocolate fork, dip each peanut truffle into the melted chocolate, covering the whole outside surface. Lift each truffle out of the chocolate and shake the fork gently up and down to let the excess chocolate drop off. Immediately roll each truffle in the crumbled paçoca until it's fully covered. (Alternatively, you can sprinkle some crumbled paçoca on the top of the truffle, immediately after dipping.) Let the chocolate fully set before removing them from the crumbled paçocas.

8   Store the truffles in an airtight plastic container in a dry place at a cool room temperature for up to 3 weeks.

CAIPIRINHA BONBONS
Bombom de Caipirinha

When I entertain, I like to develop new recipes and try them on my guests. For one dinner party, I thought of a creative way to present caipirinha in a candy. Although I use a molded bonbon technique for this recipe, you can also hand-dip them in tempered chocolate, like truffles (see Peanut Butter Truffles, page 164). If you can't find cachaça, this ganache is so good it's worth using another alcohol, like vodka. As a sign of a fine bonbon, the outer shell should not be too thick, but you can't make it too thin otherwise the shell will break. Working with good brands of chocolate is a mantra, but when it comes to making bonbons, it is pivotal. That's because a good chocolate will not only have a superb taste but also have the perfect balance between cocoa butter and cocoa solids. Too much cocoa butter makes the chocolate too thin, and too little cocoa butter, too thick. Also, different brands of chocolate behave in different ways, so once you find the one you like, stick to it. Read more about tempering chocolate on page 165.

1 pound bittersweet chocolate, chopped

6 ounces white chocolate, chopped

1 teaspoon corn syrup

⅓ cup, plus 1 tablespoon heavy cream

zest of 1 lime

3 tablespoons lime juice

2 tablespoons unsalted butter, at room temperature

2 tablespoons cachaça

2 polycarbonate bonbon molds
  (with 25 cavities each)

1 Follow the instructions on page 165 for melting two-thirds of the bittersweet chocolate for the mold. Using a ladle, divide the chocolate throughout the entire mold, filling each cavity completely. Tap the sides and bottom of the mold to remove any air bubbles trapped inside. Invert the mold back over the bowl of melted chocolate, letting all the excess chocolate drip out. Tap the sides again to help remove more excess chocolate. The amount of chocolate left in each cavity is critical to determine the finesse of the bonbon. Each cavity should be lined with chocolate but not filled.

2 Using a chef's knife, scrape the top of the mold to remove excess chocolate and turn it over so that the open cavities are facing the parchment paper. Allow the chocolate to set, 5 to 10 minutes.

3 Turn the mold over, with the cavities facing up, and let sit for another 20 minutes—the chocolate has to be set and dried before filling.

4 Meanwhile, make the ganache. Place the white chocolate and corn syrup in a bowl.

5 In a small saucepan, bring the heavy cream, lime zest and lime juice to a boil over medium heat. Immediately strain through a small sieve over the white chocolate. Let sit for a few seconds, then whisk the ganache gently.

6 Make sure the ganache is room temperature before you add the butter—you don't want the butter to melt in the ganache. Add the cachaça and whisk.

7 Pour the ganache into a pastry bag or ziplock bag. Cut a very small opening and carefully fill each cavity of the mold almost to the top, leaving enough space for a thin layer of chocolate to close the molds. Place the mold in the refrigerator and chill for 1 hour (or up to 1 day). Remove the mold from the refrigerator 10 minutes before adding the final chocolate layer.

8 Repeat the process of tempering the remaining one third of bittersweet chocolate, then ladle it equally over the filled mold, making sure each cavity is full. Lightly tap the mold to remove any air bubbles.

9 Lay the mold flat on the counter, cavities facing up. Holding it tightly with one hand, scrape the mold with the other hand in one swoop to remove any excess chocolate. Don't do this more than once, or the bottoms of the chocolates won't be smooth. If excess chocolate drips down the sides of the mold, just clean it off with a metal spatula back into the bowl.

10 Let the mold sit, cavities facing up, until the chocolate sets, 10 to 20 minutes. If necessary, chill the mold in the refrigerator for a few minutes more.

11 Invert the mold, cavity facing down, and gently tap against the countertop. The bonbons should easily fall out. Keep them in an airtight plastic container at room temperature for up to 3 weeks.

BAKED COCONUT
Cocada de Forno

=== **MAKES 4 TO 6 SERVINGS** ===

8 tablespoons (1 stick) unsalted butter, at room
    temperature

½ cup sugar

3 whole eggs

⅓ cup coconut milk

⅓ cup sweetened condensed milk

1 tablespoon Malibu rum

1½ cups unsweetened grated coconut

2 tablespoons all-purpose flour, sifted

1 24-ounce baking dish

One of my favorite dishes at Brazil a Gosto,
chef Luiza Trajano's elegant restaurant in São
Paulo, is a baked *cocada* (a coconut candy
made of coconut and sugar cut into squares)
with lemon sorbet. It is so delicious that I had
to experiment with it back in my American
kitchen. I have to admit I am very happy with
the final result and I think you will be, too.
This is an unpretentious and easy dessert to
assemble. You can prepare everything in advance and just bake it on the day of serving.

1   Preheat the oven to 350°F. Lightly grease a
    baking dish with some spray.

2   In the bowl of an electric mixer fitted with
    the paddle attachment, mix the butter and
    sugar until light and creamy at medium
    speed, about 5 minutes. Add the eggs, one
    at a time, and continue to mix. Scrape the
    sides of the bowl after each addition.

3   Add the coconut milk, sweetened condensed
    milk, and Malibu and continue to mix at me-
    dium speed until the batter is well blended,
    about 1 minute. Add the coconut and mix
    until it is all incorporated, although the batter
    will look grainy.

4   Fold the flour in with a rubber spatula.
    Spread the batter into the prepared baking
    dish. You can keep this in the refrigerator,
    covered with plastic wrap, up to 2 days
    ahead of time.

5   Bake in the oven until the top looks golden
    brown, the edges are set, but the center is
    slightly jiggly, about 20 minutes. Remove it
    from the oven and let it rest for 10 minutes.

6   Serve with a scoop of lemon sorbet.

GLOSSARY

Açaí – Açaí

Açaí's look is similar to a blueberry in color and size, with a seed the diameter of a pea. One berry holds very little pulp, but fortunately, the fruit grows like a weed on a type of palm tree with a slender trunk generally 82 feet high. Just about every part of the tree can be used: the fruit and its seeds, the roots, the hearts of palm, and the fruit stalks. But the most esteemed harvest is the fruit itself, which produces the açaí juice, extracted by a process of maceration. For cooking purposes, the fruit must be bought in its frozen pulp version, then thawed before using.

Brazil Nuts – Castanha-do-Pará

This nut comes from an enormously tall tree that can reach up to 150 feet in height, so the only way to harvest the nuts is to wait for the fruit to fall. These fruits are quite large, about the size of a cantaloupe, and each one contains between 10 and 25 nuts. The oblong nut is the part we eat and cook with, and it has a crunchy yellowish kernel with a very thin brown skin. Brazil nuts are so rich in protein that only 2 nuts are the equivalent of eating an egg. You can use the Brazil nut in a variety of recipes the way you use almonds or hazelnuts. Store them in the refrigerator or the freezer inside a ziplock bag.

Brazilian Cream Cheese – Requeijão

Brazilians are absolutely crazy for this mild flavored cream cheese. Like so many of our culinary treasures, it started back in colonial times when slaves were given sour milk. By leaving the milk to sit, the fat in the milk separates, but it's then incorporated back into the curd by slowly mixing the two together over low heat. Depending on the consistency of the requeijão, a little or a lot of milk is also added. In Brazil, one of my favorite brands of requeijão is Catupiry, available in many Brazilian stores. It's the brand I use for the recipes in this book.

Cachaça

Cachaça is a distilled beverage from Brazil, as important to the country as vodka is to Russia and tequila is to Mexico. Essentially it is an aguardente—a spirit distilled from fruits or vegetables—in this case,

the juices of the sugarcane. Cachaça is distinct from rum though, which is made from the molasses not the cane's juice. The spirit was invented in the mid-1500s in Brazil, when Portuguese colonizers began to cultivate sugarcane. Somewhere in a sugar mill around São Paulo, some stems of rough sugarcane were forgotten and yielded a foamy, nonalcoholic juice that naturally fermented. The drink had a strong effect on the body, was frequently used as a painkiller, and it was served to slaves for centuries. Eventually the Portuguese decided to distill and age it, creating a new type of aguardente and named it cachaça. There are many different kinds of wood (oak, cherry, and jequitibá rosa among them) used for aging the spirit, each leaving different traces of taste—some with a more floral flavor, others with a hint of vanilla or cinnamon.

Chayote – Chuchu or Xuxu

Chayote is a tender squash from the same family as melons, cucumbers, and squash. When handling chayote, the vegetable releases oil that sticks to our hands like wax—which is why often you'll see them individually wrapped in plastic. I simply wear gloves when handling it while other Brazilians peel it under running water.

Coconut milk – Leite de Côco

Despite the name, coconut milk contains no dairy whatsoever; the "milk" is nothing but coconut blended with hot water, then strained. Although it is quite easy to make at home, coconut milk can be found in any supermarket and has become a common pantry ingredient in the American home kitchen. Most coconut milks are sold canned or in a glass bottle and they can sit for a long time in your pantry (while the homemade version will last only a few days in the refrigerator). Make sure you shake the can or bottle well before using it. Sometimes, the coconut milk can solidify so much that shaking is not enough. In this case, place the unopened can or bottle in a bowl with hot water for 20 minutes to help liquefy it again. If your coconut milk is too thick, you can always thin it out with a few teaspoons of warm water.

Different brands of coconut milk might present a small variation in sweetness and consistency. I use a Brazilian brand, Sococo, for all my recipes because I find it has the purest taste of coconut, with less

sweetness, and the best consistency of all coconut milks. Other brands such as Goya or Thai are good, too.

Cupuaçu – Cupuaçú

Cupuaçu is a fruit that grows in the Amazon in the same family as the cacao. The pulp, which is separated from the seeds, has a very strong and alcoholic taste. Due to its high acidity, it's never consumed raw, but freezes quite well. Cupuaçu is used in Brazil in hundreds of different recipes, from mousses, ice creams, puddings, pies, and cakes. Most likely cupuaçu won't reach the American market in its true form anytime soon, but you will find cupuaçu being sold in a pasteurized and frozen form. Make the mistake of trying to eat it thawed and you'll never go near it again. Cook with the pulp, and you will, like me, fall in love with it (see my recipe on page 156). I like to buy it directly from www.kajafruit.com, or whenever I see it in the freezer of Brazilian specialty stores.

Dendê oil – Azeite de Dendê

This oil is the mainstay of Bahian cuisine, and is the product extracted from the dendê palm tree, which was brought to Brazil by African slaves, back in the seventeenth century. The dendê palm tree is one of the most oleaginous in the world, producing more oil then soybeans, peanuts, or coconut. The fruit and the pit are used in two different ways. The dendê oil used in cooking is extracted from the fruit pulp; first it is cooked in steam, then it is dried completely in the sun. The fruit is then crushed to release its bright oranged-red oil. The pit is also used to extract oil of a different kind, with a transparent color, mostly used for cosmetics for its similarity to cocoa butter. Often sediment forms on the bottom of a dendê oil bottle. To liquefy, simply place the bottle in a bowl with warm water and let it sit for 20 minutes.

Dulce de leche – Doce de Leite

This is truly a Latin ingredient produced and used all over South America. In Brazil, the state of Minas Gerais is the heart of Brazil's dairy country and the biggest producer of the best dulche de leche. Essentially, dulche de leche is milk and sugar cooked slowly until it reaches the consistency of a caramelized paste. In Brazil we eat dolche de leche in all kinds of consistencies: as a candy, as a soft paste, hard paste, more sweet, less sweet, even diet. For all of the recipes in this book, I used canned Nestlé dulce de leche.

Jerk Meat - Carne Seca
Jerk meat is a huge part of Brazilian cooking. In Portuguese we also call it *carne de sol*, referring to salt-cured and sun-dried meat. Most jerk meats come from a lean cut, such as a top round, because too much marbled fat (what gives that buttery richness we want in our cooked meats) makes the dried meat too tough. Most pieces of jerk meat are cut against the grain to make them tender rather than leathery. The processes of making American jerk beef vary greatly, from salting to brining, smoking in hickory or oak, or not smoking at all. Flavoring can be introduced with a dry rub, a paste, or a marinade. Drying can take place in commercial ovens, dehydrators, or naturally. The Brazilian method is less elaborate. While many of the ingredients found in this country are comparable to those found in Brazil, jerk meat is the exception so it might taste a little different from the one eaten in Brazil. Most Brazilian stores in the United States carry a ready-made version of prepared *carne seca* that I use in some of the recipes in this book.

Linguiça
Linguiça is a type of sausage typical from Portugal and brought to Brazil during colonial times. Today linguiça is the most adored sausage in Brazil, served in *churrascarias* (our barbecue restaurants), as hors d'oeuvres and in dishes such as *feijoada, farofa,* soups, and braises. The robust sausage is made from cured pork meat and flavored with onion, garlic, and condiments. When cooking linguiça, never poke the link, you don't want any fat to escape, as this is what makes the linguiça taste so moist and tender in the center. If you can't find it, you can use chorizo or fresh sausage as well.

Manioc Starch
Manioc starch *(povilho doce)* and sour manioc starch *(povilho azedo)* are both extracted from yucca. The vegetable is first grated, then washed and its pulp is squeezed over a bucket. The starch accumulated in the bucket is then extracted from the liquid, which is then dried and sifted. The difference between them is a natural fermentation process undergone by the sour starch

when it is left at room temperature for a period of 15 days to ferment. The manioc starch has a much finer consistency and more delicate texture than the sour manioc starch and is mostly used in sweets and crackers.

Although it may sound a little confusing, don't mistake manioc starch for manioc flour. It gets even more confusing because in English, manioc starch is usually called tapioca flour. So here are a few useful terms with quick translations:
Farinha de mandioca = manioc flour (used to make *farofa*)
Povilho doce = manioc starch = tapioca flour (used to make *pao de queijo* and other baked goods)
Povilho azedo = fermented, sour manioc starch = fermented tapioca flour, found in any Brazilian store (also used to make pao de queijo and other baking goods). Yoke is a brand widely available in the United States and Europe.

Minas Cheese
Minas cheese is to Brazil what feta is to Greece, or what mozzarella is to Italy. The taste is also a cross between a feta, a ricotta, and mozzarella. Brazilians eat Minas cheese throughout the country, but Mineiros (people born in Minas Gerais) are really proud to have created it in their state of Minas Gerais, hence the name. Minas cheese, made from cow's milk, is white, fresh, and firm. Like other fresh white cheeses, Minas has a way of complementing other flavors without masking them, and it definitely deserves more attention on its own. It is mostly consumed fresh but the cheese can also be ripened to various degrees: *fresco* (fresh), *meia-cura* (semi-ripened), and *curado* (ripened).

Plantain – Banana-da Terra
The plantain is a first cousin of the common banana. Unlike its cousin though, it cannot be eaten raw. It is larger and starchier than a banana and very versatile: It can be mashed, fried, baked, or braised. It's easy to find plantains year-round at most supermarkets, especially Latin and Asian specialty stores. You can always buy them online at retailers like Melissa's (www.melissas.com). Plantains can be used at every stage of ripeness for diverse results. When the peel is green, the flesh is very firm and starchy, almost like a potato. When the peel is semiripe, it looks yellow with lots of

black specks, and the fruit is sweeter and still starchy. When the peel is black and shriveled, the fruit is softer, less starchy, and at its sweetest.

Salt Cod – Bacalhau Salgado
Salt cod arrived on the Brazilian table through our colonizers, and today Brazil is the biggest consumer of salt cod followed by Portugal, Spain, and Italy. Brazil however, is not a producer—all our product is imported from Norway and Portugal. Brazilians rarely eat fresh cod as it's just not available to us. The Vikings were the first to learn the process of preserving fish by hanging it in the air, causing the fish to lose weight and become a hard plank—perfectly suited for transportation and trade. Once reconstituted, it presents a flaky flesh that is absolutely delicious. The best species of cod for salting is the Atlantic cod, *Gadus morhua*. When using salt cod, it's very important to desalt it properly: Use a big plastic container as the volume of water has to be at least 10 times bigger than the weight of the cod. I also like to use a rack or colander so the cod is floating completely in the water. Try to find cod that has thick flesh.

Yucca
This tuber vegetable also goes by the names manioc or cassava. Earthier tasting than a potato and richer in starch, this vegetable is one of the foundations of Brazilian cooking. It comes from a perennial shrub with origins in the Amazon. The plant's long roots grow in clusters and are covered in a thick, shiny brown skin, and a thick white layer. When cut off, the outer layers reveal a snow white, firm interior with gray or purple veins. The center of the vegetable also carries a woody fiber that is not pleasant to eat, but is easy to remove. Riper yuccas usually contain less fiber in their centers. Generally speaking, the thicker the yucca, the riper it is. There are so many derivatives of this one vegetable: toasted flour, flakes, starches, juices. Even the skin and leaves are used in some parts of Brazil. For home use, yucca is mostly boiled or fried and becomes very creamy with a mellow taste. When buying yucca, try to look for an even colored vegetable with slightly waxy brown skin and no soft or moldy spots. Many of the yuccas sold in the United States are coated with a thin layer of wax to help extend its shelf life.

INDEX

ACKNOWLDEGMENTS

This project has been in my mind for many years, but completing a book about my native country's cuisine in a second language was a stretch I wasn't quite sure I was capable of doing.

If it wasn't for the encouragement of some very special and talented people, this project wouldn't have happened. It all started when my husband Dean Schwartz introduced to me Charlie Wing, an incredible author, who is a great inspiration. He led me to Dolores York, who saw this project grow from a teeny-weeny-seed into a book. Thank you both, so much! Thanks to Jane Stern, who encouraged me to walk with my own legs, and gave me great insights all along the way.

Thanks to Alan Richman and David Leite for making me exercise the skill of writing, always coaching me with supreme technique, and helping me find a manner of therapy in writing.

Thanks to my incredible agent Joy Tutela, for helping me shape my ideas, guiding me with decency and professionalism, and for always being stable and strong during this wild ride and its many sharp turns. And to everyone at David Black Literary Agency who helped with this project, in particular, many thanks to Luke Thomas, who helped with the manuscript.

At Kyle Books, thanks to Kyle Cathie for welcoming this project into her house and to my editor, Anja Schmidt, for embracing my ideas and shaping them into this book—always with a warm and collaborative spirit.

Thanks to amazing photographers Luciano Bogado, who took many of the market shots in Brazil, and to Ben Fink, who photographed all the finished dishes. Thank you both for making this book such a visual joy. *Todos os esforços foram realizados no sentido de obter as autorizações das pessoas retratadas nas fotos originadas do arquivo pessoal da Autora; no entanto, apesar do evidente consentimento, não conseguimos localizá-las, razão pela qual estão reservados os direitos de imagem para atender eventuais futuras reivindicações.*

Thanks to Roy Finamore for his creative prop styling, and his expertise on the industry was a great contribution. Thanks to Susan Varanajan for styling the food so beautifully for the camara. Jee Chang captured the spirit and colors of Brazil into the design of this book—thanks for your beautiful work.

Thanks to recipe testers: Martha Schueneman, Cynthia Kruth, Alicia Kirchhof, Nicole Carpino, and Richard Schulman. Thanks to Chef Georges Mendes for letting me peek into his kitchen at Aldea and sharing the best *Arroz de Pato* I've ever eaten.

Obrigado ao meu maravilhoso analista José Alberto Zusman, que me ajudou a descobrir a minha verdadeira paixão pela culinaria – sua voz está sempre comigo, mesmo a muitos kilometros de distância.

Obrigado ao meu irmão e amigo Jimmy Benzaquen, a quem eu confio e consulto como uma fonte de sabedoria, sua esposa Fernanda e minha sobrinha Valentina por abençoar nossas famílias com alegria.

Obrigado a meus pais Selma e Salomon Benzaquen, que sempre me fizeram sentir amada e me apoiaram a mudar de carreira e buscar o meu sonho em outro país. Voces são os pais mais normais, estáveis, e sábios que eu conheco, e a fonte de inspiração para o jeito que eu amo os meus próprios filhos.

My husband, my best friend, my biggest supporter—Dean, who brings his laptop to the kitchen to stay with me while I am cooking the fifth version of Toucinho do Céu late at night—thanks for understanding my obsession, for embarking on this journey with me, and for your infinite love. To my children Thomas and Bianca—who are the greatest joy and the balance in my life.

I cherish my friendship with Dina Cheney, Patty Pulliam, and Arnaldo Dines—thanks for everything. It would be hard to list all of my Brazilian and American friends, with whom I have shared so many meals. Thanks for all the good times we shared together enjoying health, children, life, and so many recipes in this book. Thanks to the Riback family for your love and support since day one.

Obrigado aos feirantes de Ipanema no Rio de Janeiro pelas frutas maravilhosas.

E obrigado ao meu país- Brasil, que me fez e me faz tão feliz. E um privilégio e alegria poder representar a nossa cozinha e nossa cultura nesse livro.